The Story of My Life

CBSE Class X

English-Hindi

The Story of My Life

CBSE Class X

English-Hindi

ARIHANT PRAKASHAN, MEERUT

ARIHANT PRAKASHAN, MEERUT

All Rights Reserved

卐 **Administrative & Production Offices**

Corporate Office 4577/15, Agarwal Road, Darya Ganj, New Delhi -110002
Tele: 011- 47630600, 23280316; Fax: 011- 23280316

Head Office Kalindi, TP Nagar, Meerut (UP) - 250002
Tele: 0121-2401479; Fax: 0121-2401648

卐 **Sales & Support Offices**

Agra, Ahmedabad, Bengaluru, Bhubaneswar, Chennai, Delhi(I&II), Guwahati, Haldwani, Hyderabad, Jaipur, Kolkata, Kota, Lucknow, Nagpur, Meerut, Patna & Pune

卐 **ISBN** 978-93-5176-527-1

Typeset by Arihant DTP Unit at Meerut

For further information about the products from Arihant,
log on to www.arihantbooks.com or email to info@arihantbooks.com

Preface

The CBSE, in order to develop the habit of long-text reading in students, has introduced this novel in curriculum of class X English Communicative and English Language and Literature. This book is prescribed keeping in view the lightness of the text and simplicity of the plot of the novel so that students will enjoy reading it.

The Story of My Life, first published in 1903, is Helen Keller's autobiography detailing her early life, especially her experiences with Anne Sullivan. It records the events of Helen first twenty two years and tell us how she struggled to overcome her disabilities to learn to read, write, speak and acquire the benefits of education with the help of her teacher and life-long companion, Miss Sullivan.

This series has been specially prepared with the purpose to make the reading of novels easy and less time consuming. The novel has been covered in English & Hindi Language both because reading in English is takes more time than in Hindi. For this reason, we have tried to make the reading easy by giving the material in both Hindi & English Language, so that the students can understand the content of the novels in a comfortable way and then write the perfect answers.

We have tried to help out the students in all aspects to learn this novel in such a way so that they will become competent enough to answer the questions that will come in exams. We hope the student will relish this book.

Novel Outline

About the Novel

The Story of My Life was written while Helen Keller, then in her early twenties, was a student at **Radcliffe College**. It is a moving story of the education of a child with the extreme handicap of being deaf and blind.

The book begins with a rather vague description of young Helen's earliest memories, before she became deaf and blind at the age of nineteen months, but most of it narrates her teaching by Anne Sullivan of the **Perkins Institute** for the Blind.

The Story of My Life is far from the cry for help that it might easily have been. The tone is one of joy. Keller emphasises her early love for language. She recalls learning to speak before she lost her ability to see or hear and her desperate attempts to reawaken this ability.

Throughout the book, there is a strong emphasis on her love for language, especially the written word, which was, after all, one of the few ways she had of relating to the outside world.

The major emphasis of The Story of My Life is on the work of Sullivan, whom Helen always in this book refers to as Teacher. As subsequent writings made clearer, Sullivan's methods were far from orthodox at the time.

She communicated with Helen mostly by use of the manual alphabet, although **lip-reading** with fingers was also attempted. At the time, oral communication was almost universally stressed among educators of deaf children.

Novel के बारे में...

The Story of My Life हेलेन केलर के द्वारा तब लिखी गई थी जब वह बीस साल की थी और **रेडक्लिफ कॉलेज** में पढ़ती थी। यह एक ऐसी बच्चों को शिक्षा की कहानी है जो पूरी तरह से अंधी व बहरी थी। पुस्तक की शुरूआत युवा हेलेन की शुरूआती यादों (जो अस्पष्ट भी थीं) से होती है। उस समय वह अंधी या बहरी नहीं हुई थी तथा वह उन्नीस माह की भी नहीं थी। पुस्तक के अधिकांश हिस्से में हेलेन ने मिस सुलिवान द्वारा दी गई शिक्षा का वर्णन ही किया है जो **परकिंस इंस्टीट्यूट** से आई थी।

The Story of My Life उस मदद से कोसों दूर है जो इस तरह के बच्चे अक्सर प्राप्त करना चाहते हैं। यह खुशी के स्वर मालूम होते हैं। केलर भाषा के ज्ञान की अपनी चाह पर बल देती हुई मालूम होती है। वह अपनी बोलना सीखने की कौशल को याद करती हैं और मानती हैं कि जब वह अंधी तथा बहरी हो गई थी तो अपनी इस इन्द्री को जगाने की हर संभव कोशिश करती थी। सम्पूर्ण पुस्तक में हेलेन का भाषा के लिए प्यार झलकता है, खासकर लिखित भाषा के लिए, जिसे वह एकमात्र साधन मानती थी बाहर की दुनिया से जुड़ने के लिए।

The Story of My Life की ज्यादातर प्रमुखता सुलिवान के कार्य पर है जिसे हेलेन ने हमेशा अपनी पुस्तक में एक शिक्षक के रूप में प्रेषित किया है। आगे की लिखाई से स्पष्ट था कि सुलिवान का तरीका प्राचीन तरीकों से भिन्न था। सुलिवान ने हेलेन से ज्यादातर संवाद मैनुअल अल्फाबेट के जरिए ही किया था। **ओष्ठ-लिपि** को भी अँगुलियों से पढ़ने की कोशिश की गई थी। उस समय शिक्षाविद् मौखिक वार्तालाप को बधिर बच्चों की शिक्षा के लिए ज्यादा इस्तेमाल करते थे।

Know the **Character...**

Helen Keller

She is the main character of the book, she is blind and deaf but even with that she doesn't show any repugnance for her state, there is much to say about her like she is very close to her family specially with his mother, because she's always like talking about what she does with them and all the stuff they have done for her, Like for example when she tells that when she was young she thought that her little sister wasn't like her mom's daughter.

She was always seeing her as an intruder or something, other remarkable thing that can be mentioned about Helen Keller is that she is always trying to improve herself like she really likes to find new ways to communicate herself, for example that summer she spent practicing her French, what I can tell about her is that she is an awesome life example.

Kate Adams Keller

According to the reading, Helen's Mother was tall, blonde and had blue eyes, she helped to the family at the cotton plantation, and was always taking care of Helen this can be deducted cause she was the one who realised that beside Helen's Illness there was something wrong on her daughter, she also tried helping her daughter by reading "American Notes" From Charles Dickens' about the awesome work that had been done with some deaf and blind children she died in 1921 from an unknown illness.

Arthur H. Keller

Helen's father, in the story there is not too much about him, but what can be known of him is that he is a captain who married Kate Adams (Helen's Mother) and when they started living as a couple. He owned a cotton plantation and was the editor of a weekly newspaper. He was always taking care of his daughter, Helen liked a lot when he told some stories to her.

Mr Anagnos

Mr Anagnos was the director of the Perkins Institution. He sent Anne Sullivan to the Kellers' home. He and Keller became friends, and he had her sit on his knee when she visited the Institution. When Keller wrote "The Frost King," she sent it to him for his birthday, but because Mr Anagnos came to believe that she intentionally plagiarised it, the friendship was forever ruined.

Dr Graham Bell

Dr Graham Bell first met Keller when she was six years old and her parents brought her to him for advice on how to teach her. Dr Bell suggested that they contact the Perkins Institution for the Blind, which they did. Dr Bell remained a friend to Keller and Anne Sullivan and accompanied them on a trip to the World's Fair.

Novel में उपस्थित प्रमुख व्यक्ति

हेलेन केलर

Helen (हेलेन) इस उपन्यास की मुख्य चरित्र है। वह सुन और देख नहीं सकती, पर इसके बावजूद भी उसने इसे अपनी कमी के तौर पर नहीं व्यक्त किया। उसके बारे में कहने को बहुत कुछ है, पर वह सबसे करीब अपने परिवार के थी और खासकर अपनी माँ के। हेलेन अपनी माँ की चर्चा हमेशा करती और उन सभी का जिक्र करती, जो हेलेन ने अपनी माँ की तरफ से महसूस किया था। शुरुआत में हेलेन को उसकी छोटी बहन उसकी जिंदगी में एक अनावश्यक दखल के तौर पर महसूस हो रही थी।

हेलेन को यह भी लगता था कि वह उसकी माँ की बेटी की तरह नहीं है। हेलेन हमेशा ही अपनी जिंदगी में एक तरक्की की गुंजाइश समझती और इसके लिए पूरी जिंदगी प्रयास जारी रहा। Languages (भाषाओं) का ज्ञान भी हेलेन की सतत जद्दोजहद रही थी। वास्तव में वह एक बेहतरीन उदाहरण थी।

केट एडम्स केलर

Kate Helen (केट हेलेन) की माँ थीं और वे लंबी तथा खूबसूरत महिला थीं। घर के सभी कामों में वे मदद करती थीं और हेलेन का हमेशा से ही ख्याल रखती थीं। हेलेन की शारीरिक अक्षमता की वजह से भी उसकी माँ उसका खास ख्याल रखती थीं और यह स्वाभाविक भी था। हेलेन की माँ ने उसकी हर संभव मदद करनी चाही, ताकि हर अक्षमता को पार कर वह शिक्षा का स्वाद चख सके। हेलेन की उस बीमारी का निदान भी उसकी माँ की वजह से ही संभव हो पाया।

आर्थर एच. केलर

Arthur Keller (आर्थर केलर) हेलेन के पिता थे। कहानी में उनके बारे में बहुत चर्चा तो नहीं है, पर हेलेन की जिंदगी में उनका योगदान भी कम नहीं था। वे सेना में Captain (कैप्टन) थे तथा अपनी पत्नी के साथ रूई की पैदावार का काम देखते थे। वे एक साप्ताहिक अखबार में संपादक के तौर पर काम करते थे। वे अच्छे कथाकार थे और हेलेन उन्हें बहुत पसंद करती थी।

मि. एनाग्नॉस

Mr Anagnos (मि. एनाग्नॉस) Perkins Institute (परकिंस इंस्टीट्यूट) में निदेशक थे। उन्होंने ही मिस सुलिवान को केलर के घर भेजा था। वे और केलर अच्छे मित्र बन गए थे। जब भी एनी परकिंस जाती, तो मि. एनाग्नॉस उसे प्यार से अपनी गोद में बिठाते थे। जब एनी ने The Frost King ('द फ्रॉस्ट किंग') लिखी, तो उसे एनाग्नॉस के जन्मदिन पर भेंट किया था। बाद में एनी पर जब साहित्यिक चोरी का आरोप लगा था, तो एनाग्नॉस और एनी के बीच की मित्रता टूट गई थी।

डॉ. ग्राहम बेल

Dr Graham Bell (डॉ. ग्राहम बेल) एनी से तब मिले थे जब वह मात्र छ: साल की थी और एनी के माता-पिता उसकी शिक्षा के संबंध में सलाह लेने के लिए उसके पास आए थे। डॉ. बेल ने ही उन्हें परकिंस जाने की सलाह दी थी। डॉ. बेल आजीवन हेलेन व सुलिवान के मित्र बने रहे थे और विश्व मेले में भी उनके साथ गए थे।

The Story of
My Life

Term I

Interesting and Important Episodes in Helen's Autobiography

Helen Keller starts her life's story by suggesting that she is slightly reluctant talking about her childhood and admits that writing an autobiography is not an easy task. To avoid being boring while writing her life story Helen decides to talk about only the interesting and important episodes.

Family History of Helen

Helen was born on 27 June, 1880 in Tuscumbia, a little town in Alabama. Her grandfather Caspar Keller, a native of Switzerland had land in Alabama and settled there. Her father, Arthur H Keller was a captain in the Confederate Army and her mother Kate Adams was much younger to him.

Baptisation of Helen

As the first born in the family there is a fair amount of discussion about whom to name her after. At first her father suggests Mildred Campbell, an ancestor, but later declines to take part in the discussion. Her mother chooses Helen's grandmother's name, Helen Everett and finally her father on his way to the church gives her the name as Helen Adams.

Helen's Childhood and Miss Sullivan

Helen's house Ivy Greens was surrounded by trees, creepers, rare flowers and the fragrance of sweet flowers filled by the air. She was a happy child, but an illness, left her blind and deaf when she was 19 months old, in February. To lose her sight and hearing was like a nightmare, but, she gradually got used to the silence and darkness that surrounded her. Things changed when her teacher Miss Sullivan takes care of her and helps her spirit free.

हेलेन की जीवनी के महत्त्वपूर्ण एवं रोचक प्रसंग

Helen Keller (हेलेन केलर) अपनी जीवनी की शुरूआत में यह स्पष्ट करती है कि वह अपने बचपन के पलों को लिखने में असहज महसूस करती है और वह यह भी मानती है कि अपनी जीवनी लिखना उसके लिए आसान कार्य नहीं है। उसके लेखन में नीरसता न आए इसीलिए वह सिर्फ महत्त्वपूर्ण एवं रोचक प्रसंगों का वर्णन करने का निश्चय करती है।

हेलेन की पारिवारिक पृष्ठभूमि

हेलेन का जन्म 27 जून, 1880 को Albama (अलबामा) में एक छोटे नगर में Tuscumbia (टुसकुंबिया) में हुआ था। उसके दादा Casper Keller (कैस्पर केलर) Switzerland (स्विट्ज़रलैंड) से थे, अलबामा में अपनी जमीन होने के कारण वह वहाँ बस गए थे। पिता Arthur H Keller (ऑर्थर एच केलर) संघीय सेना में कैप्टन थे। माँ Kate Adams Keller (केट एडम्स केलर), हेलेन के पिता से उम्र में काफी छोटी थी।

हेलेन का नामकरण

परिवार की पहली संतान होने के कारण उसके परिवार में इस बात की चर्चा जोरों पर थी कि बच्चे का नाम क्या रखा जाए? पिता का प्रथम सुझाव Mildred Campbell (मिल्डर्ड कैम्पबेल) था, जो एक पूर्वज का नाम था, परंतु बाद में वह वार्तालाप से हट गए। उसकी माँ ने हेलेन की दादी माँ का नाम, Helen Everett (हेलेन एवरेट) चुना और अंततः चर्च जाते समय रास्ते में पिता ने उसका नाम Helen Adams (हेलेन एडम्स) रखा।

हेलेन का बचपन और मिस सुलिवान

हेलेन का घर Ivy Greens (आइवी ग्रीन्स) पेड़, बेलों, दुर्लभ फूलों से चारों तरफ से घिरा हुआ था और हवा फूलों की मीठी सुगंध से भरी हुई थी। वह एक खुश बच्ची थी, फरवरी में जब वह 19 माह की थी, एक बीमारी ने उसको अंधा और बहरा बना दिया। अपनी देखने और सुनने की क्षमता खो देना उसके लिए दुखद स्वप्न की तरह था, लेकिन धीरे-धीरे उसको अपने चारों तरफ अँधेरे और चुप्पी की आदत हो गई। हेलेन के लिए परिस्थितियाँ तब बदलने लगती हैं जब Miss Sullivan (मिस सुलिवान) उसकी देखभाल करने लगती हैं।

Word Meaning

Superstitious	– अंधविश्वास	Veil	– पर्दा, घूँघट	
Fantasy	– कल्पना	Vividly	– जीवंत	
Poignancy	– मार्मिक	Tedious	– कठिन कार्य	
Vital	– महत्त्वपूर्ण	Ancestors	– पूर्वज	
Deprived	– वंचित	Homestead	– रहने की भूमि	
Annex	– सहायक भवन	Reluctant	– इच्छा न होना	
Clematis	– फूल का पौधा	Nightmare	– बुरा स्वप्न	
Fragile	– नाजुक	Resemble	– के समान दिखना	
Asphodels	– लिली फूल की एक किस्म	Disposition	– व्यवस्था बनाना	
Imitating	– नकल करना	Impulse	– प्रबल इच्छा	
Dreary	– उदासी से भरा	Agony	– पीड़ा, कष्ट	
Bewilderment	– उधेड़बुन, उलझन			

Important Questions

Questions based on the Plot of the Chapter

Q 1. Why is there a fear in the mind of Helen Keller to write the history of her life?

अपनी जिंदगी के इतिहास को लिखने में हेलेन किस डर को महसूस कर रही थी?

हेलेन को डर महसूस होना – उसका अपनी निजी जिंदगी के बारे में न बताना – हेलेन का सोच लेना कि आत्मकथा लिखना मुश्किल होगा – हेलेन का सोचना कि लिखी हुई चीजें प्रभावपूर्ण नहीं होंगी – लोगों की दिलचस्पी न होना

Ans. There was a fear in the mind of Helen regarding writing the autobiography. It was because of the superstition that she had about unveiling the life. Moreover she was a bit reluctant because writing her autobiography seemed tedious to her. Another fact that, she had in her mind was that if her writing became boring then it would take away the pleasure of reading. All these things were restraining her from writing her autobiography.

Above all this, her life had not been so joyous that she could rejoice at it. She had been a victim of the loss of sight and hearing ability. This might have given a feeling to the readers of her writing that all the writings were trash and there was not be anything amusing at all. Even, this would have been a reason of her aversion towards not writing her autobiography with an ease. Helen must have all these fears in her mind and that's why she was resisting all her desire for writing the piece.

Q 2. How and why was she named Helen? Narrate the naming incident.

हेलेन को उसका नाम कैसे मिला? नामकरण से जुड़ी घटना को वर्णित करें।

परिवार में पहली संतान का नामकरण के लिए विचार करना – पिता ऑर्थर एच केलर के सुझाव को अस्वीकार करना – माता केट एडम्स के सुझाव पर हेलेन का नाम दादी माँ की शादी से पूर्व वाला रखने का फैसला करना – चर्च जाते समय पिता ऑर्थर एच केलर का तय किया हुआ नाम भूल जाना – हेलेन को नाम मिल जाना।

Ans. There is an interesting episode behind the naming of Helen. She was the first child in the house so a lot of discussion was going on for name. Suggestion of Arthur H Keller (Helen's Father) was not accepted and he left the lot. Kate Adams (Helen's Mother) suggested a name of Helen's grandmother. When Arthur H Keller was going to church, he forgot the maiden name of the grandmother and Helen got the other one.

The way it all went on was a lot funny and it had got all the elements of the pure jocularity. It all started with the suggestion of the father. He proposed a name and it was readily rejected. When he felt that the rejection is indication of failure then he left the whole conversation and set off.

Finally, the female members of the house continued the discussion and they came up with a specified that was of the name of Helen's grandmother and it was decided then to be the name of Helen. Hence, she got her name.

Helen's Sign Language

After Helen loses her hearing and sight, she tries to communicate with others by using crude signs. However, she could understand quite a bit of what was going around her. Once when she felt the shutting of the door, she knew that guests had arrived and she went to her room to change into a formal dress. She realises that she is different from others and her handicap makes her quite angry and frustrated at times.

Helen's Friends – Martha and Belle

Her closest friends were Martha Washington, the cook's daughter and Belle, her dog. They spent a great deal of time together in the kitchen, the sheds and the stables and many a time Helen bossed over Martha and gets away with it. Once, Martha got too naughty and chopped off Helen's curls with a pair of scissors while cutting out paper dolls.

Helen's Close Shave with Fire

One day when Helen wets her apron and she tries to dry it near the fire place, she gets too close to the hot ashes and gets burnt. Viny, the old nurse, saves her just on time.

Helen's Mother is Locked in Pantry

Helen learnt to use the key and as a prank locked her mother in the pantry for three hours. Helen enjoys as her mother pounds on the door and the other member cannot hear anything as they are in other parts of the house.

हेलेन की सांकेतिक भाषा

अपनी देखने और सुनने की क्षमता को खो देने के बाद Helen (हेलेन) ने दूसरों के साथ बातचीत करने के लिए सांकेतिक भाषा का इस्तेमाल करने की कोशिश करती थी, हालाँकि वह अपने चारों तरफ क्या चल रहा है, थोड़ा-थोड़ा समझती थी। एक बार जब उसने दरवाजे के खुलने की आवाज सुनी, तो उसे आभास हो गया कि मेहमान आए हैं और वह कपड़े बदलने के लिए अपने कमरे में चली गई। उसे लगा कि वह अन्य लोगों से भिन्न है और अपनी इस अपंगता पर कई बार उसे बहुत क्रोध भी आता था।

हेलेन के दोस्त-मार्था और बेल

हेलेन के सबसे करीबी दोस्त Martha Washington (मार्था वाशिंगटन), जो उसके रसोईया की बेटी थी और Bell (बेल), जो उसका कुत्ता था। वे दोनों ही घंटों तक अपने खेल में व्यस्त होते और रसोईघर, बगीचे और अस्तबल आदि में घूमते रहते थे और हेलेन हर वक्त मार्था पर अपने आदेश थोपती रहती और मार्था बिना इंकार किए उसकी कही बातें मानती। एक बार, मार्था बहुत शरारती हो गई और उसने कागज की गुड़िया काटते समय कैंची से हेलेन के बाल काट दिए थे।

हेलेन का आग से सामना होना

एक दिन जब हेलेन का Apron (एप्रन) गीला हो गया तब वह उसे आग के पास सुखाने की कोशिश में गर्म राख के काफी पास तक पहुँच जाती है और जल जाती है। ठीक समय पर उसकी पुरानी नर्स Viny (विनी) ने उसे बचा लिया।

हेलेन की माँ का पेन्ट्री में बंद होना

हेलेन को चाबी का इस्तेमाल करना आ गया और मजाक में उसने एक दिन अपनी माँ को तीन घंटे के लिए Pantry (पेन्ट्री) में बंद कर दिया। हेलेन आनंद ले रही थी, क्योंकि उसकी माँ दरवाजा खोलने की आवाज लगा रही थी, परंतु घर के बाकी सदस्य उसकी आवाज सुन नहीं पा रहे थे क्योंकि वे घर के दूसरे हिस्सों में थे।

Word Meaning

Clung	– चिपक जाना	Crude	– अपरिष्कृत, कच्चा, नया
Shivered	– काँपना	Distinguished	– अलग-अलग पहचान
Vague	– अनिश्चित	Anointed	– तेल मलना
Enormous	– बहुत ज्यादा	Bustle	– चहल-पहल
Dangled	– झूलना	Hem	– कपड़े का किनारा
Vexed	– चिंतित	Frantically	– बेतरतीब ढंग से
Exhausted	– थका हुआ	Akin	– एक समान
Setter	– कुत्ते की एक प्रजाति	Seldom	– शायद, कभी-कभी
Domineer	– वर्चस्व स्थापित करना	Tyranny	– तानाशाही
Kneading	– आटा गूँथना	Prattle	– आवाज
Swarmed	– भिनभिनाना	Gobbler	– लालची के जैसे खाने वाला
Retribution	– बदला	Guinea fowl	– अफ्रीका में पाया जाने वाला एक पक्षी
Emphatic	– दबाव देना		
Curiosity	– जिज्ञासा	Delight	– खुशी
Tidbit	– स्वादिष्ट भोजन	Mischief	– शरारत
Fuzzy	– मुलायम और कोमल	Wearied	– थक जाना
Clipping	– मजबूत सतह	Honey suckle	– फूल की एक किस्म
Quivered	– काँपना	Rigid	– कठोर
Contemptous	– घृणा दिखाना	Hearth	– भट्टी
Suffocated	– दम घुटना	Detached	– अलग करना
Pounding	– जोर से मारना	Jar	– कंपन्न
Prank	– मजाक	Induced	– राजी करना
Drift	– विचलन	Indulgent	– अति उदारवादी
Caressing	– प्यार से छूना	Acquired	– हासिल करना
Clumsily	– अनजान तरीके से	Indelicate	– असभ्य
Intruder	– घुसपैठ	Victim	– शिकार
Presumption	– पूर्वनुमान	Solitude	– एकांत, शांति
Endearing	– पसंद किया जाना	Caprice	– अनुमान करना

Important Questions

Questions based on the Plot of the Chapter

Q 1. How did Helen communicate with others during the first months after she lost her eye-sight and hearing?

अपनी सुनने और देखने की क्षमता खोने के बाद हेलेन ने प्रारंभिक दिनों में बातचीत कैसे की?

↗ अपनी सुनने और देखने की क्षमता खोने के बाद हेलेन के लिए बातचीत करना मुश्किल हो जाना – हेलेन का सांकेतिक भाषा का प्रयोग करना – माँ को बुलाने के लिए कपड़े पकड़ना – आईसक्रीम के लिए हेलेन का काँपने जैसा मुश्किल कार्य करना।

Ans. It was very tough for Helen to communicate with others, when she lost her eyes and her hearing power. She used to pull her mother's clothes to call her. A push was meant for go and a pull was meant for come. Whenever she needed an ice-cream, she would shiver and would mimic the way ice-cream was made. This was not very easy, but Helen had to cope up with all that difficulties. One can understand what a big challenge it would be for someone, who has lost his two important senses.

Basically what Helen used to do as a way of communication was using her other senses. She had developed some gestures too as she had to depend upon that. Also, she must have strived hard to get away of communication. As we have already known that her communication skills were very limited, so she encoded some prominent signs for herself and those were quite understandable by the family members. That's how she talked in her early days.

Helen's Zest for Communication

Helen realised that to express herself, she needed to work harder and learn more ways to communicate with others. In her effort to do so, she often got impatient and frustrated. She often loses her temper. Sometimes these outbursts occurred every hour of the day.

Helen's Mother is Hopeful

Her mother's only hope is from Charles Dickens, 'American Notes' in which she read about 'Laura Bridgman', the first deaf-blind person to receive a formal education under Samuel Howe at the Perkins Institute. When Helen was six years old, her father heard of a well-known oculist in Baltimore and with her parents, Helen went to meet him.

Journey to Baltimore

During the journey, she plays with a string of shells, the conductor's ticket punch and a doll made of towels. This toy was given to her by her aunt, but it had no eyes, nose, mouth or ears. Helen felt that the doll needed eyes, so she pulled two beads from her aunt's cape and expressed to her aunt to sow them as eyes on the doll's face. In Baltimore, they met Dr Chisholm, a specialist in diseases and disorders of the eyes, but he was unable to do anything about Helen, he suggests they should meet Dr Alexander Graham Bell (the inventor of the telephone and a teacher of the deaf) in Washington.

Meeting with Dr Graham Bell

Helen found Dr Bell's company comforting and Dr Bell advised her father to write to Dr Anagons, Director of Perkins Institute in Boston. In reply to the letter, Dr Anagons conveyed that a teacher Miss Sullivan would come to teach Helen.

हेलेन की बात करने की चाहत

Helen (हेलेन) को महसूस होने लगा कि अन्य लोगों से संवाद करने के लिए उसे और मेहनत करके कुछ और तरीके खोजने पड़ेंगे। इस वजह से वह कभी-कभी परेशान और नाराज हो जाती। वह अक्सर गुस्से में आ जाती थी। कभी-कभी ऐसा दिन में हर घंटे होता था।

हेलेन के प्रति माँ की आशा

उसकी माँ की एकमात्र आशा Charles Dickens 'American Notes' (चार्ल्स डिकिन्स की 'अमेरिकन नोट्स') थी, जिसमें हेलेन की माँ ने किसी लेख में मूक-बधिर बच्ची 'Laura Bridgman' ('लाउरा ब्रिजमैन') के बारे में पढ़ा था, जिसने Samuel Howe (सैमुयल हैवे) से Perkins Institute (परकिंस इंस्टीट्यूट) में औपचारिक शिक्षा प्राप्त की थी। जब हेलेन छ: साल की थी तो हेलेन के पिता ने Baltimore (बाल्टमोर) में किसी प्रसिद्ध नेत्र विशेषज्ञ के बारे में सुना था, हेलेन अपने माता-पिता के साथ उनसे मिलने गई।

हेलेन की बाल्टमोर यात्रा

यात्रा के समय वह कंडक्टर की पंचिंग मशीन तथा तौलिए से बनी Doll (गुड़िया) से बहुत देर तक खेलती रही। यह गुड़िया हेलेन को उसकी Aunt (चाची) ने दी थी, जिसमें आँखें, कान, मुँह और नाक नहीं थीं। हेलेन ने महसूस किया कि गुड़िया को आँखों की आवश्यकता है, इसलिए उसने अपनी चाची की केप से दो मोती खींचे और अपनी चाची को व्यक्त किया कि उनको गुड़िया के चेहरे पर, आँखों की तरह लगा दिया जाए। बाल्टमोर में वे Dr Chisholm (डॉ चैसलोम) से मिले जो आँखों के विशेषज्ञ थे, परंतु वह उनकी सहायता नहीं कर सकते थे, डॉ चैसलोम ने उन्हें Washington (वाशिंगटन) में Dr. Alexander Graham Bell (डॉ एलेक्जेंडर ग्राह्म बेल) (टेलीफोन के आविष्कारक तथा मूक बधिरों के शिक्षक) से मिलने की सलाह दी।

डॉ ग्राह्म बेल के साथ मुलाकात

हेलेन को डॉ बेल का साथ आनंदमय लगा और डॉ बेल ने उसके पिता को बोस्टन में परकिंस इंस्टीट्यूट के संस्थापक व निदेशक Dr Anagons (डॉ एनागॉन्स) को पत्र लिखने को कहा। पत्र के उत्तर में एनागॉन्स ने Miss Sullivan (मिस सुलिवान) का नाम सुझाया और कहा कि वे हेलेन को पढ़ाने आएँगी।

Word Meaning

Desire	– इच्छा	Adequate	– पर्याप्त
Invariably	– न बदलने वाला	Out bursts	– गुस्सा
Passion	– लगाव	Resistance	– प्रतिरोध
Miserable	– दयनीय	Tempest	– भयंकर तूफान
Grieved	– दु:खी होना	Perplexed	– उलझा हुआ
Eminent	– जाना–पहचाना	Contented	– संतोष होना
Amused	– आश्चर्यचकित	Provoking	– उकसाने वाला
Persistency	– बरकरार रखना	Tumbled	– लड़खड़ाकर गिरना
Cape	– बिना बाजू वाला कोट	Energetically	– उत्साहपूर्वक
Misgivings	– डर, भय	Unconscious	– बेसुध
Anguish	– पीड़ा, दु:ख	Endeared	– पसंद आने का कारण
Pleasure	– खुशी	Tenderness	– कोमलता
Sympathy	– सहानुभूति	Admiration	– प्रशंसा
Isolation	– अलगाव	Companionship	– एक–दूसरे का साथ होना
Competent	– सक्षम	Assurance	– भरोसा
Sacred	– पवित्र	Vision	– दृष्टिगोचर

Important Questions

Questions based on the Plot of the Chapter

Q 1. Why were Helen's parents worried and confused?

हेलेन के माता-पिता चिंतित क्यों थे?

हेलेन द्वारा देखने और सुनने की क्षमता को खो देना – हेलेन का कुछ कूट संकेतों का प्रयोग करना – संकेतों का प्रयोग करने के बाद भी दिक्कतों का सामना करना – उसके माता-पिता का भी इस वजह से चिंतित रहना – माता पिता का चिंतित रहना कि किस प्रकार हेलेन की समस्या का हल निकाला जा सके।

Ans. Helen was a girl who had lost her ability to see and hear. It had made her life a big nuisance as she was unable to communicate with anyone. She had developed some crude signs by herself, but that was not enough. As she was growing, she was feeling the desperate need for communication. Her parents were observing this very closely and they were worried and confused as to how it could be made possible for her to communicate with others.

This made her parents worried and confused. In such a situation where a child is unable to use two prominent senses. It is obvious that parents become worried when their loving child loses the ability to see and hear, the intensity of lament and grief that the parents feel can be well understood.

Q 2. Narrate Helen's journey from her hometown to Baltimore.

अपने गृहनगर से बाल्टमोर की यात्रा हेलेन ने कैसे की? वर्णन करें।

हेलेन अपने माता-पिता के साथ बाल्टमोर की यात्रा पर जाना है – ट्रेन की यात्रा में हेलेन को दो खिलौने मिलना – एक तौलिए से बनी गुड़िया और दूसरा कंडक्टर की पंचिंग मशीन – तौलिए वाले खिलौने में हेलेन द्वारा आँख लगाने की जिद करना – कंडक्टर की मशीन से हेलेन का घंटों तक खेलना – हेलेन की यात्रा का बहुत उत्साहपूर्ण होना।

Ans. When the worry of Helen's parents was over about all the possible consequences then it was decided by them to have a visit to Baltimore, where they were supposed to see Dr Graham Bell. They boarded a train and it was a lot of fun for Helen. In the way, Helen was given a doll made up of towel by her aunt. Helen played a lot with that doll and insisted upon putting up beads for the eyes. she had another toy in the form of the punching machine of the train conductor which the conductor allowed willingly for her.

She did a lot with the available two toys. Finally, they met Dr Graham Bell in Baltimore, who was very helpful to Helen and her parents. This journey was more meaningful to Helen than to her parents. This journey was aimed at the better life prospects for Helen and this journey was really wonderful and later on it proved its worth in her life.

4

The Most Important Day in Helen's Life Arrival of Miss Sullivan

On 3rd March, 1887, when Helen was six years and nine months old, her new teacher Anne Mansfield Sullivan came to teach her. Helen considered this day the most important in all her life and realised that something unusual was going to happen, even before Miss Sullivan arrived, from the activities of the people in her house. As Helen eagerly waited for her guide and teacher to arrive, she hoped that light would come into her life through all the mist. She compared her situation to a ship moving in dense fog, trying to reach the harbour.

First Moment of Miss Sullivan's Arrival

As Miss Sullivan came towards Helen, she stretched her hands and held it close to hers. Helen got a sense of relief as now there was someone to tell her about the new things in life and most important, she would also receive love.

Miss Sullivan Gifts a Doll to Helen

The blind children at Perkins Institute sent a doll for Helen as a gift through Miss Sullivan. While playing with the doll, Miss Sullivan spelt "d-o-l-l" on Helen's hand and in the following days she learnt to spell some more words like pin, cup, hand, sit, stand and walk.

However, all this required patience and once there was confusion over the words "m-u-g" and "w-a-t-e-r". Repeated attempts to make Helen understand resulted in an outburst and Helen threw her doll at her feet. She however, did not feel sorry for the broken doll as she did not love this doll.

४

हेलेन के जीवन का सबसे महत्त्वपूर्ण दिन मिस सुलिवान का आना

3 मार्च, 1987 को जब Helen (हेलेन) छ: वर्ष नौ महीने की थी तब उसकी नई शिक्षक Anne Mansfield Sullivan (एने मैंसफिल्ड सुलिवान) उसको पढ़ाने आई। हेलेन ने इस दिन को अपने जीवन का सबसे महत्त्वपूर्ण दिन माना और लिखा है कि Miss Sullivan (मिस सुलिवान) के आगमन से पहले घर में काफी अच्छा माहौल था और इसी वजह से हेलेन को ऐसा लग रहा था कि उसके घर में कुछ अप्रत्याशित होने वाला है। हेलेन ने उत्साहित होकर अपनी गाइड और शिक्षिका का इंतजार किया और उसे आशा थी कि उसके जीवन के रास्ते से धुंध हटकर प्रकाश आने वाला है। उसने इसकी तुलना एक जहाज को Dense Fog (घने कोहरे) में किनारा ढूंढने से की।

मिस सुलिवान के आगमन का प्रथम पल

जैसे ही मिस सुलिवान हेलेन के पास आई तो उन्होंने उसके हाथों को फैलाकर हेलेन को अपने से चिपका लिया। हेलेन को आराम का अहसास हुआ, क्योंकि अब उसे जीवन की नई चीजों के बारे में बताने के लिए कोई था और सबसे महत्त्वपूर्ण बात यह भी कि वह उनसे प्रेम भी प्राप्त कर सकेगी।

मिस सुलिवान का हेलेन को एक गुड़िया उपहार में देना

Perkins Institute (पर्किंस इंस्टीट्यूट) के नेत्रहीन बच्चों ने मिस सुलिवान को हेलेन के लिए एक गुड़िया उपहार में दी जब हेलेन उस Doll (गुड़िया) से खेल रही थी, तो मिस सुलिवान ने हेलेन के हाथों में "d-o-l-l" लिखा और कुछ ही दिनों में हेलेन ने पिन, कप, हैंड, सिट, स्टैण्ड और वॉक जैसे शब्दों को सीख लिया। इसके पश्चात् मिस सुलिवान ने हेलेन को "m-u-g" और "w-a-t-e-r" में भेद बताने का प्रयास किया था, परंतु हेलेन उलझन में इन दोनों चीजों को एक ही मानती थी। इससे हेलेन अधीर हो गई और बाद में गुस्से की वजह से हेलेन ने वह गुड़िया उनके पैरों में फेंक दी। हेलेन को गुड़िया के टूटने का अफसोस नहीं हुआ, क्योंकि वह शायद इस गुड़िया को प्यार नहीं करती थी।

Miss Sullivan Takes Helen Outside the House

Miss Sullivan took Helen outdoors to the well-house, where she taught her the meaning of water. By touching the cold water, Helen realised that everything had a name and each name gave birth to a new thought. When she came home, she realised what she had done to her doll and tried to put the broken pieces of the doll back together. She cried and for the first time, she felt sorrow and repentance.

मिस सुलिवान का हेलेन को घर से बाहर ले जाना

मिस सुलिवान हेलेन को बाहर एक कुएँ के पास ले गईं, जहाँ उन्होंने उसे पानी का मतलब सिखाया। ठण्डे पानी को छूकर हेलेन को लगा कि प्रत्येक चीज का एक नाम होता है और प्रत्येक नाम एक नए विचार को जन्म देता है। जब वह घर वापस आई उसे अहसास हुआ कि अपनी गुड़िया को तोड़कर उसने गलती की है और उसने गुड़िया के टूटे हुए टुकड़ों को दोबारा जोड़ने की कोशिश की। वह रोने लगी और उसे पहली बार खेद और पश्चाताप का अहसास हुआ।

Helen Learns More Words

Helen learnt more words like mother, father and sister and considered herself the 'happiest child' and looked forward to a new day so that she could learn more.

हेलेन का नए-नए शब्द सीखना

हेलेन ने और भी शब्द सीखे ; जैसे-माता, पिता और बहन और वह अपने आप को सबसे ज्यादा Happiest Child ('खुशकिस्मत बच्ची') मानने लगी और नए दिनों की प्रतीक्षा करने लगी, जिससे वह ज्यादा शब्दों को सीख सके।

Word Meaning

Immeasurable–	जिसे मापा न जा सके	Contrast	– विरोधाभास
Eventful	– घटनाओं से भरा हुआ	Porch	– छज्जा
Dumb	– बेजुबान	Expectant	– उम्मीद करना
Vaguely	– अनिश्चित रूप से	Penetrated	– प्रतिच्छेद करना
Lingered	– ज्यादा देर तक रुकना	Unconsciously	– बेसुध
Marvel	– सुखद	Preyed	– शिकार किया जाना
Languor	– थकान	Tangible	– जिसे छूकर देखा जा सके
Tense	– तनावपूर्ण	Anxious	– उत्सुक
Groped	– महसूस करना	Plummet	– औंधे मुँह गिरना

Important Questions

Questions based on the Plot of the Chapter

Q 1. Why was 3rd March, 1887, the most important day in Helen's life?

3 मार्च, 1887 हेलेन की जिंदगी का सबसे महत्त्वपूर्ण दिन क्यों है?

↙ 3 मार्च, 1887 का दिन हेलेन की जिंदगी का महत्त्वपूर्ण दिन होना – हेलेन की शिक्षक मिस सुलिवान का इस दिन उसके घर आना – उनके आने की वजह से ही हेलेन का शिक्षित होना – अत: इस दिन वास्तव में महत्त्वपूर्ण होना।

Ans. The life of a man is worth only when he has been equipped with the rapier of education that cuts all the barriers of the life and makes it a real one. A man has to gain the education and needs to apply it so that he could excel himself in the field of life. On the same ground of argument, we can say that 3rd March, 1887 was the most important day in Helen's life. It was because of the fact that Miss Sullivan, her teacher arrived the same day to her house to teach her. Only by then, Helen would be flourishing in her life and could be able to make herself a great success. Considering all these facts, we can say that the day was really important to Helen. Another reason for this day to be important is that Helen had remembered this day by heart even the day was of her early childhood. If someone is remembering the day with so much of affinity then the day must be really important to the person.

Q 2. What makes Helen throw the doll which Miss Sullivan had gifted her?

हेलेन ने वह खिलौना क्यों फेंक दिया, जो मिस सुलिवान ने उसे उपहार स्वरूप दिया था?

↙ मिस सुलिवान के आने के बाद हेलेन को शब्द सिखाए जाना – मिस सुलिवान का हेलेन को 'm-u-g' और 'w-a-t-e-r' सिखाने की कोशिश करना – हेलेन को ये दो शब्द समझ नहीं आना – मिस सुलिवान की लगातार कोशिशों के बावजूद भी हेलेन का न सीख पाना – मिस सुलिवान का अगले दिन भी हेलेन को वो दो शब्द सिखाने की कोशिश करना – लेकिन कुछ भी सकारात्मक नहीं होना – गुस्से की वजह से हेलेन ने वह खिलौना, जो उसे उपहार में मिलना, जमीन पर गिरा देना।

Ans. After the arrival of Miss Sullivan, Helen was getting the lessons over the words, its spellings, etc. A day Sullivan was trying to make Helen familiar with the words, 'm-u-g' and 'w-a-t-e-r'. Miss Sullivan tried her level best to let her know, but all was in vain. Sullivan tried it on a fresh day so that she could be able to do that but none comes as a result. In that very frustration, Helen threw her doll on the floor and the doll was broken down into fragments.

All this happened but there was no sign of any kind of grief on the face of Helen for doing this. The fact is very much clear that Helen had often had a fit of temper and she would lose her control then. When she was in that condition then she would throw anything that comes her way. The same had happened in the case of the doll that Helen broke deliberately.

Q 3. How was the 'Mystery of Language' revealed to Helen? Explain how the experience makes her happy and confident.

हेलेन को 'भाषा का रहस्य' कैसे पता चला? इससे हेलेन को खुशी और आत्मविश्वास कैसे प्राप्त हुआ?

मिस सुलिवान का हमेशा ही कुछ नए शब्दों को सिखाने की कोशिश करना – हेलेन द्वारा भाषा सीखने की बहुत ज्यादा इच्छा रखना – भाषा को सीखने के पश्चात् ही अपने आसपास की चीजों को बेहतर समझना – दौड़कर अपनी माँ के पास जाना और उनके सामने सीखे हुए शब्दों को पुनः प्रदर्शित करना – उसके उत्साह से खुशी और उसका आत्मविश्वास दोनों प्रदर्शित होना।

Ans. Miss Sullivan always tried to teach Helen a new word in order to reveal the mystery of language, but it gave immense pleasure to Helen and Sullivan both. Since, Helen was in a desperate need of learning a new way of communication and Sullivan helped her thoroughly. When Helen got to know a few words then she was happy from the bottom of her heart. She gyrated in glee and ran to her mother. She did the same trick of words that her teacher had taught her in these recent days.

She was making the expression of imitating the words she had known by then. This reveals her happiness and confidence. When Helen felt that she was being so much able to understand others then the pleasure that she had got from it was beyond any explanation. Then she got to know the lying beauty and mystery of the language.

Q 4. How does Helen compare her life to that of a great ship?

हेलेन को अपनी तुलना एक बड़े जहाज से करने की चारित्रिक विशेषता क्या थी?

मिस सुलिवान का हेलेन के घर में आने की सूचना से पूरे घर में उत्साह का माहौल होना – हेलेन का इन चीजों को महसूस करना और सोचा कि उसकी नई शिक्षक कैसी होगी? – मन में कई तरह के ख्याल आना और हेलेन का परेशान होना – हेलेन द्वारा समुद्र में फँसे एक जहाज से अपनी तुलना करना।

Ans. It was the time of arrival of Miss Sullivan, Helen's teacher to her house. It was a very great day to her as well as for her whole family.

As it seems evident, when a guest is to arrive, there remains a great bustle all around the house and the same was noticed in the house. The expectations were big and there was a great going-on in the minds and hearts of Helen.

Thoughts were switching on and off as it happens when someone is going to meet a strange man. She compared herself to that of a very big ship.

Which has been in the sea and get caught in the storm. Every now and then, there remains a thinking what is going to be the next? So, was the case with Helen.

That's why she compared herself with that of a big ship.

Helen Explores with Her Hands Nature and All its Aspect

Recalling many incidents of the summer of 1887, Helen spends a lot of time exploring with her hands and learning the name of every object that she touched. This made her happy and more confident as she could now communicate with the people around her.

Miss Sullivan Takes Her to the Fields

When the season of daisies, Miss Sullivan took Helen to the fields and taught her how plants grew from the sun, how birds build their nests and how other animals the squirrel, the deer and the lion find food and shelter. She linked Helen's earliest thoughts with nature and made her feel that the birds and flowers were happy peers.

Helen's Unkind Experience with Nature

One day, Miss Sullivan helped Helen climb a tree where Helen sat on a shaded branch. Miss Sullivan then went to the house to fetch lunch for Helen. Suddenly, there was a thunderstorm which made Helen very scared as broken branches fell on her. She tried to save herself from falling off. Miss Sullivan saves her just on time and when Helen is on the ground; she promises not to ever climb a tree.

The Mimosa Tree Attracts Helen

The mere thought of climbing a tree fills Helen with terror, until one spring morning the fragrance from a full mimosa tree attracts her and she is tempted to climb it. As she climbs the tree, she finds a little seat among the branches and sits on it. This makes her happy and now she realises that there are bad times and good times in a person's life.

हेलेन का प्रकृति और उसके भावों को हाथों से समझना

1887 ई. में गर्मियों में होने वाली घटनाओं को ध्यान में रखते हुए यह कहा जा सकता है कि Helen (हेलेन) अपना ज्यादातर समय हाथों की गतिविधियों में तथा प्रत्येक स्पर्श की गई वस्तु का नाम सीखने में बिताती है। इन बातों से वह खुश होती थी तथा वह और आत्मविश्वासी हो गई, क्योंकि अब वह अपने आस-पास के लोगों से सवाल कर सकती थी।

मिस सुलिवान का हेलेन को घर के बाहर ले जाना

जब फूलों का मौसम आया तो, Miss Sullivan (मिस सुलिवान) हेलेन को मैदान में ले गई और उसे बताया कि किस तरह पौधे धूप से बढ़ते हैं, चिड़िया अपना घोंसला कैसे बनाती हैं, कैसे दूसरे जीव गिलहरी, हिरण, शेर अपना भोजन और आश्रय प्राप्त करते हैं, वह हेलेन के विचारों को प्रकृति के साथ जोड़ती हैं और उसे अहसास कराती हैं कि चिड़िया और फूल एक दूसरे के साथ खुश रहने वाले साथी हैं।

हेलेन को प्रकृति के क्रूर रूप का आभास होना

एक दिन, मिस सुलिवान हेलेन की पेड़ पर चढ़ने में मदद करती है, जहाँ हेलेन एक छायादार शाखा पर बैठ जाती है। तब मिस सुलिवान हेलेन के लिए खाना लेने के लिए घर चली गई। तभी अचानक से, एक भयंकर तूफान आया जिससे हेलेन अत्यधिक डर गई इतने में पेड़ की कमजोर डालियाँ उस पर टूट कर गिरने लगीं। उसने अपने आप को नीचे गिरने से बचाने का प्रयास किया। मिस सुलिवान समय पर आई और उन्होंने उसे बचा लिया और जब हेलेन नीचे आई तो उसने वादा किया कि अब वह कभी पेड़ पर नही चढ़ेगी।

हेलेन का मिमोसा के पेड़ से आकर्षण होना

तूफान की वजह से जो डर हेलेन के मन में पैदा हुआ था वह इतनी आसानी से निकलने वाला नहीं था, परंतु Spring Season (वसंत ऋतु) में एक दिन मिमोसा के पेड़ को देखकर हेलेन को गजब का आकर्षण हुआ और उसने Mimosa (मिमोसा) के पेड़ पर चढ़ने की इच्छा जताई। पेड़ पर चढ़ने के बाद दो डालियों के बीच उसे एक छोटी-सी जगह मिली और वह उसी पर बैठ गई। उस दिन वह बहुत खुश हुई और अहसास हुआ कि एक इंसान की जिंदगी में अच्छे और बुरे दोनों तरह के पल आते हैं।

Word Meaning

Incident	– घटनाएँ		Awakening	– जगाना
Explore	– तलाश करना		Joyous	– खुशी–खुशी से/खुशहाल
Kinship	– भाईचारा		Beneficence	– लाभकारी
Pleasant	– खुशनुमा		Thrive	– समृद्ध होना
Fragrant	– खुशबूदार		Peers	– सहयोगी/सहकर्मी
Ramble	– घूमना		Sultry	– बेहूदगी/बेकार
Grateful	– कृतज्ञ		Scramble	– चढ़ पाना
Luncheon	– खाना		Precedes	– आगे बढ़ना
Clutched	– पकड़ लेना		Immense	– बहुत ज्यादा
Enfolded	– गले लगाना		Expectant	– उम्मीदवार
Sinister	– दुष्ट		Shiver	– कँपकपी
Swayed	– हिलना-डुलना		Strained	– मजबूती से बँधा हुआ
Impulse	– प्रबल इच्छा		Crouched	– पैर मोड़कर बैठना
Lashed	– अचानक गति करना		Intermittent	– बीच-बीच में होना
Treacherous	– धोखा देना		Mere	– केवल
Allurement	– आकर्षण		Subtle	– मुलायम, कोमल
Instinctively	– जन्मजात गुण		Exquisitely	– बेहतरीन तरीके से
Delicate	– सौम्य		Paradise	– स्वर्ग
Transplanted	– दूसरी जगह ले जाना		Irresolute	– हिचक होना
Forked	– फैला हुआ		Delicious	– स्वादिष्ट
Fairy	– परी		Rosy	– गुलाबी
Fair	– सही, उचित			

Important Questions

Questions based on the Plot of the Chapter

Q 1. Narrate Helen's experience which taught her that nature is not always kind.

हेलेन के उस अनुभव का वर्णन कीजिए, जिससे यह पता चलता हो कि प्रकृति हमेशा उदार नहीं होती।

↙ हेलेन का अपनी टीचर के साथ बाहर घूमने जाना – उसे प्रकृति का हर रूप अच्छा और प्यारा लगना – एक पेड़ ने हेलेन को आकर्षित किया और अपनी शिक्षक की मदद से हेलेन का पेड़ पर चढ़ जाना – मिस सुलिवान का भोजन के लिए घर जाना – इसी बीच एक भयंकर तूफान द्वारा माहौल को अस्त-व्यस्त कर देना – उस समय हेलेन के डर का कोई अंत न होना – उसका जल्दी-से-जल्दी अपने शिक्षक को वहाँ से उतारने के लिए बुलाना – इस घटना से हेलेन को यह पता चला कि प्रकृति हमेशा उदार नहीं होगी।

Ans. Once Helen was out for a nice strall with her teacher Miss Sullivan. They went to a garden and watched a lot of things, nature's beauty, flora and fauna and a lot more.

The fact that Helen got to know from this event is that nature has bestowed upon man all the goodness and all the benevolence. So, Helen was very happy about all this. When she went further she was fascinated by a tree and she insisted to climb that tree.

Miss Sullivan took her request readily and they both climbed the tree. After a while, Miss Sullivan went home to bring lunch and Helen stayed there.

Suddenly a tempest gathered round and brought about almost a havoc. Branches crumbled down and fell down. Helen was afraid and she wished Miss Sullivan to come there. Finally, she was saved by her teacher but, she got to know nature is not always kind.

Q 2. What made Helen overcame her fears of climbing a tree? What did experience make her arouse?

पेड़ पर चढ़ने के डर पर हेलेन ने कैसे विजय प्राप्त की? इस अनुभव ने उसे क्या सिखाया?

प्रारंभ में हेलेन का पेड़ पर चढ़ने का अनुभव अच्छा न होना – उसकी शिक्षक द्वारा हेलेन को जीवन के बारे में समझाना – प्राकृतिक घटना को जीवन की घटना की तरह सोचना – जीवन के अलग-अलग पहलुओं को समझना

Ans. The very first experience of Helen climbing the tree was not viable to Helen. She was in a deep trouble and she wished not to get caught in such situations further. She got to know the disasterous face of nature. But her teacher taught her that we must learn how to cope up with the difficulties that often come by in the lives. We must endure and we must fight it back.

It will do a lot good to us. As nature is friendly, it is hostile too and such is the life where we have to face sorrow at times as we often anticipate happiness for ourselves. She then, overcomes her fear of climbing the tree. By this experience, she learnt about the life and its oddities that may come. The learning was somehow philosophical for Helen. She could not have learnt these things otherwise. She must be grateful to the nature that offered her such great chance of learning the things for herself.

Q 3. What did the narrator say that it was a long time before she climbed another tree? What new lesson did she learnt about nature?

कथाकार ने ऐसा क्यों कहा कि उसे दूसरे पेड़ पर चढ़ने के लिए बहुत ज्यादा वक्त लगा? प्रकृति के बारे में उसे क्या सीख मिली?

पेड़ पर चढ़ने से हेलेन के मन में डर बैठना – हेलेन की शिक्षक का उसकी प्रकृति के रूप समझाना – सभी विषयों को समझाने में हेलेन का काफी समय लेना – सभी विषयों को समझने पर हेलेन का जिंदगी के नए पाठ को अनुभव करना – हेलेन को समझ आना कि, उसे जिंदगी के एक नए पाठ को सीखने का अनुभव हुआ।

Ans. Helen was deeply disturbed by the fear that she had after climbing the tree. She used to have the fear on a very consistent basis and she can't deny it. She thought that nature is having a killer instinct. She was on the wrong side of the thought. Her teacher tried to console her thought by saying that at times nature may be hostile, but all these were not instantly enough for Helen to let herself get the relief.

What she had got to know that there are two faces of nature one is appealing and the other is appalling. She took her own time to comfort herself about these thoughts and when she fully comprehend the thoughts, she got back to the climbing of tree. She learnt the due lesson of life by this incident.

People often learnt a lesson from the nature and so was the case with Helen. It was a long time for sure, but it could not be termed to be an idle one. Helen got to know the character of nature then.

Q 4. What did the narrator do after she climbed the mimosa tree?

मिमोसा के पेड़ पर चढ़ने के बाद कथाकार ने क्या किया?

हेलेन का मिमोसा के पेड़ की ओर आकर्षित होना – उसका पुराना डर दूर हो जाना – हेलेन का पेड़ के बीच में बैठना – पेड़ पर बैठने के पश्चात् नयी खुशियों का अनुभव करना।

Ans. One day Helen got attracted towards the mimosa tree and she wished to climb it. By then, she had overcome her fear of climbing the tree and she was more confident. She went and climbed that mimosa tree.

When she had done with the climbing then she managed to seat herself between a fork and then she was at the top of the world. she felt that she was amidst the cloud and she had got a pair of wings and she could fly high with all her aspirations turn rosy.

It was a feeling that had no ending and she would foster it forever. She had drowned herself into a good world of dreams and there remained only the good thoughts with her till the end.

This was just panoromatic and exhilarating sense of joy for Helen. She wished she was a bird that had got the freedom of measuring the limits of the sky. Everything was just melodramatic totally.

Helen's Vocabulary Grows

Helen now had the key to all language and looked forward to use it. It was a very difficult and slow process for a child to learn language and thus, communicate with other. As Helen's vocabulary grew, she started asking questions to her teacher.

The Meaning of Love

One morning Helen gave Miss Sullivan a bunch of violets, Miss Sullivan kissed her and spelled into her hand, 'I love Helen'. Helen wanted to know the meaning of love but was confused and puzzled because she could not touch 'love' and thus, was not able to understand it. Finally, one day when there were clouds in the sky, Miss Sullivan explains, 'love is something like the clouds'. Miss Sullivan told her that, as you cannot touch the clouds, you cannot touch love too. However, you can feel the rain and know how glad the flowers and the thirsty earth are on a hot day. Miss Sullivan treats Helen like a child who can only hear.

Miss Sullivan—A Name Synonymous with Patience

Right from the beginning of Helen's education, Miss Sullivan speaks to Helen her as she would to any hearing child; the only difference into Helen's hand instead of speaking them. This process of teaching continued for years as a deaf and dumb child does not learn in a month or even two to three years. Miss Sullivan patiently taught Helen who was both deaf and blind. This was because she can't distinguish tone of voice and can't see the speaker's face.

Helen Started Communication

When Miss Sullivan filled Helen with a confidence, she tried to start up a conversation with the rest of her family members. Yet, it was difficult a bit in the beginning but as the time passed on, she managed to communicate well.

हेलेन की शब्दावली का विकास

Helen (हेलेन) के पास लगभग सभी भाषाओं की कुंजी थी और वह इसका इस्तेमाल करना चाहती थी। मूक और बधिरों के लिए किसी भाषा को सीखना एक मुश्किल व धीमी प्रक्रिया होती है और इसी कारण उनके लिए दूसरों से संवाद करना कठिन होता है। जैसे-जैसे हेलेन का शब्द ज्ञान बढ़ा, उसने अपनी अध्यापिका से प्रश्न पूछने शुरू कर दिए।

प्यार का अर्थ

एक सुबह Miss Sullivan (मिस सुलिवान) को हेलेन ने फूलों का गुलदस्ता दिया, मिस सुलिवान ने उसे किस किया और इसके हाथों पर I love Helen (मैं हेलेन को प्यार करती हूँ) लिखा। हेलेन 'प्यार' का अर्थ समझना चाहती थी, परंतु वह समझ नहीं पाई, क्योंकि 'प्यार' को स्पर्श नहीं किया जा सकता था और इसलिए हेलेन उसे समझ नहीं सकती थी। एक दिन जब आसमान में बादल थे तब मिस सुलिवान ने हेलेन से कहा कि Love is Something Like the Clouds (प्यार कुछ बादलों के जैसे होता है)। मिस सुलिवान ने उसे बताया जैसे तुम बादलों को नहीं छू सकती, वैसे ही 'प्यार' को भी नहीं छू सकती। हालाँकि हम बारिश को महसूस कर सकते हैं और जान सकते है कि बारिश होने पर फूल तथा गर्मी के दिन में प्यासी धरती कितनी खुश होती हैं। मिस सुलिवान हेलेन के साथ एक बच्चे की तरह पेश आती हैं, जो केवल सुन सकती है।

मिस सुलिवान–धैर्य का दूसरा नाम

हेलेन की शिक्षा के प्रारंभिक दौर से ही मिस सुलिवान ने उसे एक ऐसे बच्चे की तरह पढ़ाया जैसे वह सुन सकती हो, केवल अंतर यह था कि हेलेन के सुनने की क्षमता भी उसके हाथों के स्पर्श पर निर्भर करती थी। पढ़ाई का यह सिलसिला लगातार कई सालों तक चलता रहा, क्योंकि अंधे और बहरे बच्चे कुछ महीनों में नहीं सीखते, यहाँ तक कि दो या तीन साल में भी नहीं। मिस सुलिवान हेलेन को, जो अंधी तथा बहरी दोनों थी, धैर्यपूर्वक सिखाती थी। वह आवाज के तरीकों में अंतर नहीं समझ सकती तथा बोलने वाले के चेहरे की मुद्रा नहीं देख सकती।

हेलेन का संवाद शुरू कर देना

जब मिस सुलिवान ने हेलेन को विश्वास से भर दिया इसके बाद हेलेन ने अपने घर के सदस्यों से संवाद करने का प्रयास शुरू कर दिया। प्रारंभ में उसे थोड़ी दिक्कतें आई, परंतु बाद में उसने घर के बचे सदस्यों से अच्छी तरह से से संवाद करना शुरू कर दिया।

Word Meaning

Acquire	– हासिल करना	Delightedly	– खुशी
Stammered	– हकलाना	Syllable	– शब्दों की सबसे छोटी इकाई
Vague	– आंशिक,	Inadequate	– अपर्याप्त
Revived	– पुनर्जीवित होना	Engraved	– कठोर सतहों पर लिखना
Violets	– एक प्रकार का फूल	Conscious	– सजग
Puzzled	– उलझन होना	Warmth	– गर्माहट
Disappointed	– निराश	Stringing	– गूँथना
Symmetrical	– समानता	Obvious	– निश्चित रूप से
Sequence	– क्रम	Concentrated	– ध्यान लगाना
Emphasis	– दबाव देना	Perception	– समझ होना
Abstract	– सन्निहित	Splendour	– शानदार
Intercourse	– बातचीत	Imitation	– नकल
Stimulates	– उत्तेजक	Spontaneous	– उसी क्षण
Denied	– मना करना	Ventured	– हिम्मत करना
Initiative	– शुरुआत	Appropriate	– उपयुक्त
Amenities	– सुविधाएँ	Augmented	– बढ़ाया जाना
Distinguish	– अंतर करना	Gamut	– पूर्ण शृंखला
Significance	– महत्त्व		

Important Questions

Questions based on the Plot of the Chapter

Q 1. Why was it difficult for Helen to understand the meaning of 'love'. How does Miss Sullivan finally explain it to her?

'प्यार' का अर्थ समझ पाना हेलेन के लिए क्यों मुश्किल था? मिस सुलिवान ने अंततः उसे प्यार का अर्थ कैसे समझाया?

↳ हेलेन का शब्दों को स्पर्श करके सीखना – मिस सुलिवान द्वारा हेलेन को प्यार शब्द को समझाना – मिस सुलिवान का बारिश द्वारा हेलेन को प्यार का मतलब बताना।

Ans. Helen learnt by touch whatever she learnt. If the touch is not there it was difficult for her to learn a new word. One day, Helen gifted Miss Sullivan a violets and Miss Sullivan replied with 'I love Helen'.

Helen got confused as she was unable to know what was love Miss Sullivan tried her best to teach her 'love' but all was in vain.

Miss Sullivan could not let her know that love cannot be touched and thus, she was failing. But one rainy day when there was cloud in the sky then Miss Sullivan told Helen that you can see the cloud, but cannot touch it so as with the 'love' which cannot touched.

After this incident, Helen got to know about 'love'. This longer process must have irritated both; Miss Sullivan and Helen, but it was such a good way to let the things known that Helen might not forget ever and the facts of that kind must be well-known to her everafter.

Q 2. How difficult is it to teach conversation to a child who cannot see and hear and to a child who can see and hear? Compare.

बातचीत की कला को सिखाना मुश्किल होता है। एक मूक-बधिर और एक सामान्य बच्चे के संदर्भ में इसकी तुलना कीजिए।

मूक-बधिर बच्चों को सीखने में कठिनाइयों का सामना करना – सामान्य बच्चे का शीघ्र चीजों को सीखना – शिक्षकों के लिए सामान्य बच्चों को सिखाना आसान होना।

Ans. If a child is having the visual and hearing disability then it is really very tedious for a teacher to teach such a child. Someone learns by the use of senses, but someone who has lost his two of the senses then how would a teacher be able to induce the desired knowledge in him.

It is very difficult for a child to learn even, but on the other hand a child with all his senses wide open can learn things pretty easy.

A teacher can be in a position to impart the desired knowledge in him very well using illustrative examples to the child. But real effort has to be made for a teacher, who has to deal with such a child, who is having disability with him.

As it is known that learning things is not so easy and if the learner is challenged then one can imagine how tough it is to be even for the teacher too. The input of the knowledge in such a person is an act that is beyond imagination.

Q 3. What did the narrator say about the deaf and the blind people?

मूक-बधिरों के बारे में कथाकार ने क्या कहा?

↗ कथाकार का स्वयं मूक-बधिर होना – मूक-बधिर बच्चों को सांत्वना देना – मूक-बधिर बच्चों का शीघ्र समाज की मुख्य धारा में न आ पाना।

Ans. It is very obvious that the narrator, herself, being a deaf and blind would always have a very soft corner for deaf and blind. She had quoted that a loss of hearing and visual ability cannot be compensated ever or cannot be compared to any other losses. They are suffering from the greatest loss in the world. Narrator had also said that the process of learning becomes very difficult, for such children and the hope of coming into the mainstream of society becomes very figmented for such children.

Overall, narrator had mentioned the oddities of the lives of deaf and dumb and advocated the soft corner for them. Also, they need special care from the other people also and they are a subject of complete mercy. They are the deprived children, who had been a victim of the direct situations. Therefore, the advocacy of having a soft corner for them is justified.

Q 4. What examples did Miss Sullivan use to show what love meant?

प्यार के अर्थ को समझाने के लिए मिस सुलिवान ने क्या उदाहरण दिए?

↗ हेलेन के लिए 'प्यार' का अर्थ समझ पाना मुश्किल होना – मिस सुलिवान का हेलेन के हृदय पर हाथ रखकर समझाने की कोशिश करना – हेलेन उन्हीं चीजों को समझना, जिन्हें वह स्पर्श कर सके – मिस सुलिवान द्वारा हेलेन को प्यार शब्द के लिए बादल का उदाहरण देना।

Ans. The episode of Helen's zest for understanding 'love' has a comical approach. Since, Helen has the ability to understand the words only when there is an element of touch involved but 'love' cannot be touched.

Miss Sullivan gave her an example by the touch of the heart, but Helen didn't get the example and she insisted upon the understanding, but all in vain. Then Miss Sullivan gave her the example of rain and cloud. She told her when there is rain, how happy the plants and flowers are! One cannot touch cloud, but one can see it. So, is the case with love that cannot be seen by anyone.

Love is an eternal feeling that is governed by heart and the conscience of mind. So, the way Miss Sullivan dealt with Helen for letting her understand the feeling of love was truly a superb act.

Q 5. **What did Miss Sullivan patiently explain to the narrator?**

मिस सुलिवान ने धैर्यपूर्वक कथाकार को क्या सिखाने की कोशिश की ?

मिस सुलिवान में इच्छा शक्ति का होना – मिस सुलिवान का कठिन कार्य को आसान करना – हेलेन को बादलों की मदद से प्यार का अर्थ समझाना – मिस सुलिवान की इच्छा शक्ति से परिचित कराना।

Ans. Miss Sullivan had a very big heart and above that a big determination. She was a figure of what we call patience. She had never been agitated with the constant series of questions from Helen, but she remained calm and composed all the time.

She had shown a great character when she was to deal with the understanding of 'love' but she never gave up.

Instead, she was constantly varying her examples and ideas so that Helen can be able to learn what her teacher was trying for. She had elaborated and put up efforts in a very different manner so that the things could be easier for Helen.

Nonetheless, she never lost her patience. The result of that patience came out as the perfection of Helen in her life. The attempts made by Miss Sullivan in doing the good for Helen was great success for her.

Helen Picks up Words Quickly

Helen learnt to read and as soon as she could spell a few new words, Miss Sullivan gave her slips of cardboard on which words were printed in raised letters. Helen could pick up words quickly and she had a frame in which she could arrange the words in little sentences. Learning with Miss Sullivan was interesting and special for Helen.

Helen and Miss Sullivan Studied Mostly Out of Doors

Helen and Miss Sullivan read and studied out of doors most of the time and Helen was given lessons on History, Geography and many other subjects. She made raised maps in clay, so that she could feel the mountain ridges and valleys and followed the rivers with her fingers. Helen however did not enjoy Arithmetic; later Helen even learnt Zoology and Botany.

A Gentleman sent a Collection of Fossils

Once a gentleman whose name Helen did not remember, sent her a collection of fossils. Now, she learnt about the pre-historic period too. Miss Sullivan also taught her about the creatures of the sea. Through a lily plant, Helen learnt about the growth of a plant.

Eleven Tadpoles in a Glass Bowl

There were eleven tadpoles in a glass bowl and Helen would put her hand into the bowl to feed them. She also observed how tadpoles turn into frog and make peculiar noises in summer.

हेलेन का शब्दों को तेजी से समझना

Helen (हेलेन) ने पढ़ना सीखा और जल्द ही उसने कुछ नए शब्दों को सीखा, इसलिए Miss Sullivan (मिस सुलिवान) ने हेलेन को एक Cardboard (कार्डबोर्ड) का टुकड़ा दिया, जिस पर शब्द उभरे हुए थे। हेलेन शब्दों को जल्दी से उठा सकती थी और उसके पास एक फ्रेम था, जिसमें वह शब्दों की छोटे वाक्यों में व्यवस्था कर सकती थी। मिस सुलिवान से हेलेन को पढ़ना और चीजें सीखना बहुत अच्छा लगता था।

मिस सुलिवान और हेलेन ज्यादातर घर के बाहर पढ़ते थे

हेलेन और मिस सुलिवान ज्यादातर समय घर के बाहर पढ़ते थे और हेलेन को इतिहास, भूगोल और कई दूसरे विषय पढ़ाए जातें थे। मिट्टी का इस्तेमाल कर मिस सुलिवान उसे मानचित्र बनाकर देती, जिससे वह Mountains, Ridges, Valleys and Rivers (पहाड़ की चोटियों, घाटियों तथा नदियों) को अपनी अँगुलियों से स्पर्श करके महसूस कर सके। हेलेन को गणित बिल्कुल भी पसंद नहीं था, परंतु बाद में उसने वनस्पति और जीव विज्ञान जैसे विषयों को भी सीखा था।

एक सज्जन के द्वारा जीवाश्म भेजा जाना

एक सज्जन ने, जिनका नाम हेलेन को ठीक तरह से याद नहीं, उन्होंने हेलेन को Fossils (जीवाश्म) का एक संकलन भेजा। अब वह पूर्व ऐतिहासिक काल को भी सीख सकती थी। मिस सुलिवान ने भी उसे समुद्री जीवों के बारे में बताया। Lily (लिली) फूल के एक पौधे से हेलेन को पौधों की वृद्धि के विषय में जानकारी प्राप्त हुई।

एक कटोरे में मेंढक के ग्यारह छोटे-छोटे बच्चे

काँच के एक कटोरे में छोटे-छोटे Tadpoles (मेंढक) के ग्यारह बच्चे थे और हेलेन उस कटोरे में अपना हाथ डाल देती और उसके आवागमन को महसूस करती। वह अनुसरण करती कि कैसे एक छोटा बच्चा एक युवा मेंढक में तब्दील होकर गर्मी के दिनों में शोर करता है।

Helen gives Credit to Miss Sullivan

As Helen learnt a lot of things from life itself, she gave credit to her teacher's initial years of education which were so beautiful. Helen strongly felt that any teacher can take a child to the classroom, but not every teacher can make him learn. Miss Sullivan had become a part of Helen's life and all her wisdom and knowledge was given to her by teacher.

हेलेन मिस सुलिवान की शुक्रगुजार थी

हेलेन ने अपने जीवन से बहुत सी चीजें सीखीं, जिनका सम्पूर्ण श्रेय उसने अपनी शिक्षिका से ज्ञान प्राप्त करने वाले प्रारंभिक दिनों को दिया, जो बहुत ही खुशनुमा दिन थे। हेलेन यह भी मानती थी कि एक शिक्षक बच्चे को स्कूल तक तो ले जाता है, परंतु उसके अंदर ज्ञान प्रत्येक शिक्षक नहीं भर सकता। मिस सुलिवान हेलेन के जीवन का एक हिस्सा बन चुकी थी और उसका सारा ज्ञान और बुद्धि उसके शिक्षक द्वारा दी गई है।

Word Meaning

Pinafore	एक प्रकार का पहनावा	Earnestly	गंभीरतापूर्वक
Illustrated	वर्णन करना	Dread	डर
Plodding	मेहनत करना	Precious	कीमती
Peculiar	विचित्र	Description	वर्णन
Nagged	डाँटना	Resinous	चिपचिपा
Odour	खुशबू	Gracious	दयालु
Reedy	पतली-दुबली	Downy	नीचे की जमीन
Fuzzy	फूला हुआ	Soughing	धीरे-धीरे
Devious	बेईमान	Accomplished	पूरा होना
Conscience	अंत: आत्मा	Leisurely	फुर्सत के समय में
Antediluvian	पुरातन समय	Beast	जंगली जानवर
Primeval	पुराना	Gigantic	विशालकाय
Dismal	बेचारगी	Swamp	दलदल
Gloomy	उदासी	Somber	अँधेरा
Hoof	खुर	Lustrous	चमकदार
Plolyps	एक प्रकार का जीव	Dwelling place	निवास स्थान
Isles	द्वीप	Symbolical	प्रतिरूप
Slender	छरहरा	Reluctant	इच्छा न होना
Reveal	साबित करना	Rapidly	तेजी से
Pomp	भव्यता	Doffed	उड़ान भरना

Important Questions

Question based on the Plot of the Chapter

Q 1. How did Helen learn to form sentences?

हेलेन ने वाक्य बनाना कैसे सीखा?

↙ हेलेन के लिए वाक्य संरचना का मुश्किल कार्य होना – हेलेन का स्पर्श द्वारा सीखना – मिस सुलिवान द्वारा हेलेन को उभरे हुए शब्द दिया जाना – रुचिकर तरीका होना

Ans. Drafting a sentence was not very easy for Helen. She had to put all her best efforts in order to learn the art of making a sentence. Since, Helen learnt everything by touching so Miss Sullivan provided her with the cardboards having raised letters that represented a single word. Miss Sullivan gave Helen certain words and arranged them in such a way that comprised a sentence in itself. Helen loved the way she was made to learn how to write a sentence. She also kept an object on the surface of an object and then a sentence is framed.

Sentence formation was a continuous and a very tiring process. Helen was determined even then to learn this art. Miss Sullivan did her best to procure the desired output.

Q 2. Helen and Miss Sullivan spent many happy hours and played at learning Geography. Explain.

हेलेन और मिस सुलिवान घंटों एक साथ भूगोल सीखने के दौरान कैसे खेलते थे? वर्णन करो।

↙ हेलेन की शिक्षा ज्यादातर घर से बाहर होना – पार्क या घर का बगीचा उपयुक्त होना – वनस्पति व उससे जुड़ी चीजें सीखना – चिकनी मिट्टी से बने मानचित्र – नदी व घाटी की संरचना – खेल-खेल में पढ़ाई होना।

Ans. The beautiful part of Helen's education was that Miss Sullivan used to take her out of the house for learning. They used to go to the park and gardens where they learnt about the flora and vegetation. They used to have a map made out of clay with raised and lowered designs so that Helen could understand the mountains, rivers and valleys with ease. They studied with fun involved in it.

Christmas- A Great Event

The school children of Tuscumbia invited Helen on Christmas Eve. The Christmas tree was beautifully lit up and Helen happily danced around it. There were gifts for everyone and Helen's friends threw hints to her about her gifts.

Christmas Eve-Very Restless for Helen

Helen hanged her stocking so that Santa Claus could keep his gifts in it. She was unable to sleep, but pretended to be asleep. In the morning, she woke up everyone and wished them. There were presents all over.

Helen's Favourite Gift- Tim (the Canary)

Amongst all the gifts that Helen received, the Canary, Miss Sullivan presented her, was Helen's favourite. She named it Tim and took good care of it. She prepared its bath every morning, cleaned its cage and filled its cups with fresh seeds and water.

A Cat Preyed on Tim

One morning Helen left the cage on the window-sill and on her return, she tried to feel Tim, but realised that a big cat had eaten the poor bird. This made Helen extremely sad, because she lost the Canary and Helen would never get to see her 'sweet little singer again'.

क्रिसमस–एक बड़ा दिन

Tuscumbia (टुसकुंबिया) के स्कूली बच्चों ने Christmas (क्रिसमस) की शाम पर Helen (हेलेन) को आने का आमंत्रण दिया। क्रिसमस के पेड़ को बहुत अच्छी तरह से रोशनी से सजाया गया था और हेलेन खुशी से उसके चारों तरफ नाचती रही। प्रत्येक बच्चे को उपहार दिया गया और हेलेन के सभी दोस्त उसे उपहार को पहचानने के लिए संकेत प्रदान कर रहे थे।

क्रिसमस की पूर्व संध्या–हेलेन के लिए बेचैनीभरी

हेलेन ने अपना थैला अपने कमरे में लटकाकर रख दिया, ताकि Santa Claus (सेंटा क्लॉज) उसमें उपहार रख सके। वह सोने में असमर्थ थी, लेकिन उसने सोने का नाटक किया। वह सुबह सो कर उठी, तो उसने सबको जगाया तथा बधाइयाँ दीं। चारों तरफ ढेर सारे उपहार थे।

हेलेन का सबसे मनपसंद उपहार–टिम (द केनरी)

हेलेन को प्राप्त सभी उपहारों में से The Canary (द केनरी), जो उसे मिस सुलिवान ने दिया था, उसे बहुत ही पसंद था। हेलेन ने उसका नाम Tim (टिम) रखा और वह उसकी देखभाल पूरे ध्यान से करती थी। प्रत्येक सुबह वह उसको स्नान कराती, उसका पिंजरा साफ करती और उसके कप में बीज और ताजा पानी भरती थी।

बिल्ली के द्वारा टिम को खा लिया जाना

हेलेन ने पिंजरे को एक दिन खिड़की के किनारे पर रख दिया था और उसके वापस आने पर उसने टिम को महसूस करने की कोशिश की, लेकिन उसे लगा कि एक बड़ी बिल्ली उसकी चिड़िया को खा गई है। यह हेलेन के लिए एक दु:खद घटना थी, क्योंकि उसने अपनी चिड़िया को खो दिया था और अब हेलेन कभी भी पुन: अपनी Sweet Little Singer Again (प्यारी गायक चिड़िया) को महसूस नहीं कर पाएगी।

Word Meaning

Mystery	– रहस्य	Surrounded	– घिरा होना
Delight	– खुशी	Amusement	– आश्चर्य
Curiosity	– जिज्ञासा	Pretended	– बहाना बनाना
Ablaze	– प्रज्वलित	Shimmering	– चमकदार
Capered	– खुशी से उछलना	Ecstasy	– उमंग, उत्साह
Tantalising	– उम्मीदें जगाना	Persuaded	– राजी करना
Content	– संतोष होना	Stumbling	– लड़खड़ाना
Wrapped	– लिपटा हुआ	Canary	– पीले पंखों वाली एक चिड़िया
Candied	– चीनी से बना	Chickweed	– एक प्रकार का खरपतवार
Realise	– महसूस करना		

Important Questions

Questions based on the Plot of the Chapter

Q 1. How did Helen take care of the Canary?

हेलेन केनरी का ख्याल कैसे रखती थी?

↗ केनरी हेलेन को मिस सुलिवान द्वारा दिया गया उपहार – हेलेन का सर्वाधिक टिम को पसन्द करना – उसका पूरा ख्याल रखना – खाने, नहाने का प्रबन्ध करना – हेलेन का टिम के लिए समर्पित होना।

Ans. Canary was gifted to Helen by her teacher Miss Sullivan. Canary was named as 'Tim' by Helen. She loved this gift most. Out of all the other gifts that Helen had she cared for Tim the most. She would take care of it. She would feed Tim, arrange bed and bathe him. She would not let a moment pass without the thinking of Tim. He was like an integral part of her. She paid all her attention to that singing little bird. She was, in a sense, very devoted to Tim.

Since, Tim was the most loved of all the other gifts so it was Helen's centre of attention. It was the most compassionate being for Helen. She would think that the bird should have gifted to her much earlier than, it actually was gifted. She was in complete love with the bird and when she lost the bird she was at a sense of loss and grief for it about.

Q 2. Explain how the narrator felt about the gifts she received on Christmas Eve?

क्रिसमस के मौके पर उपहार पाकर कथाकार को कैसा लगा?

↳ क्रिसमस का त्यौहार का हेलेन के लिए नई अनुभूतियाँ होना – टुसकुंबिया स्कूल से आमन्त्रण मिलना – क्रिसमस पर ढेर सारी खुशियाँ मिलना – उपहारों का आदान व प्रदान – असीम आनंद का अनुभव होना।

Ans. Christmas was packed with surprises for Helen. Not only grand, but the surprises were more than that. At first, she was invited to the school at Tuscumbia by the students. When she reached there she found that the whole school was lighted for the christmas and there was joy all around the territory. All the students were being amiable to Helen and she was overwhelmed with this feeling of closeness.

She gifted all the children there and she too received a gift in return. After receiving the gifts from different people she felt the sense of happiness that comes from mutual give and take.

Moreover when Helen received the gifts from different people she made an association with them too. This association was not only the internal bond of feeling, but also a deep and satisfying act too. She was overjoyed with the feeling of receiving and the love being shown by the persons so involved in doing that.

Q 3. What happened the next morning when the narrator woke up the entire family?

क्रिसमस की सुबह जब कथाकार ने पूरे घर को जगाया, तो क्या हुआ?

↳ क्रिसमस की पूर्व संध्या पर हेलेन द्वारा थैला खुला रखना – हेलेन का सोने का नाटक करना – घर में अगली सुबह सबसे पहले उठना – घर के सदस्यों को जगाना – असीम खुशी होना।

Ans. The day before christmas was equally significant for Helen. She had kept her stockings hung in her room before going to bed. She was expecting that Santa Claus would come and fill her stockings with numerous gifts.

She didn't get to sleep, but pretended to fall asleep. But in the morning she was the one, who got up first and she woke up all the family members in the house. But when she was on her way to the rooms of her parents. She was tumbling due to the lots of gifts that had been kept only for Helen.

She found her stockings to be filled with lots of new gifts and she was very happy on receiving the gifts. In a nutshell, when the narrator woke up the house then the sight, which she could not see unfortunately, was exhilarating. Her thought of receiving gifts from Santa Claus was fulfilled in the end. She could feel the fresh blow of emotions that had been poured into her from the multiple dimensions.

Q 4. How did Helen's friends and family make the christmas a memorable one for Helen?

हेलेन के दोस्तों और परिवार वालों ने क्रिसमस को एक यादगार दिन कैसे बना दिया ?

हेलेन को परिवार और दोस्त प्रिय होना – हेलेन के लिए क्रिसमस को यादगार बनाना – हेलेन को स्कूल में आमंत्रित करना – उसे खूब सारे उपहार प्रदान करना – परिवार द्वारा क्रिसमस को यादगार बनाना – ढेर सारे उपहार देना – हेलेन का प्रसन्न होना।

Ans. Helen was deeply loved by her family and friends. All of them were very fond of Helen. So, they were trying to make christmas for Helen a memorable one. Friends of Helen invited her to the school where she exchanged lots of gifts with her friends. The family members were also steps ahead and they prepared lots of surprises too.

They kept the stockings of Helen full of gifts and the passages of Helen's house were filled with the gifts. When Helen woke up early in the morning, she found herself tumbling around as all the gifts were for her. By this way, Helen's christmas was made to be a memorable one for her.

Friends and family both came to be a living Santa Claus for Helen showering the flush of gifts that she was anticipating in the previous night. They all gave her so many gifts that her feelings had no limit and it was beyond description.

Questions based on the Character Sketch

Q 5. Give a character-sketch of little Tim.

टिम का चरित्र चित्रण करें।

↗ टिम पीले पंखों वाली एक चिड़िया का नाम होना – टिम एक गाने वाली चिड़िया होना – हेलेन को मिस सुलिवान द्वारा एक उपहार देना – शरारती और चंचल चिड़िया का होना – हेलेन को चिड़िया बहुत प्रिय होना – हेलेन को यह अनुभव कभी भी खत्म न होने वाले आनंद की तरह होना।

Ans. Tim was a yellow feathered bird that was gifted to Helen on her best day of christmas by her teacher Miss Sullivan. It was a bird that sang so beautifully that everybody could be engrossed in its singing.

It was really playful, a naughty one and filled with energy. This bird became a playmate for Helen. She was even dedicated to the bird for its beauty and its features.

Tim was really entertaining to Helen and she used to spend hours of her day with that bird. Unfortunately, the bird met its tragic end as it was eaten up by a cat. It made Helen extremely sad for that little bird.

That singing bird was the best part Helen had in her life. Her concern for the bird was worthy of applause. The bird meant a lot to her and she did her best for the bird in respect of care and affection. In short, Tim and Helen complemented each another and that bond was of affection and emotions.

9

Helen's Visit to Boston

In May, 1888, Helen's visit to Boston was important for her. The train journey, along with her mother and teacher Miss Sulivan was different from the earlier train journey to Baltimore.

Nancy, Helen's Doll Gets Shapeless

On their arrival to Boston, the laundress gives Nancy (Helen's Doll) a bath as she was dirty. After the bath, only a formless heap of cotton remains excepting for the two beads of the eyes which look at Helen disappointedly.

Boston City - a Beautiful Fairy Tale

On Helen's arrival at Boston city she feels her beautiful fairy tale has come true. As soon as they arrive at the Perkins institution for the blind, Helen makes friends and is happy as they too communicate in Helen language of touch.

Visit to Bunker Hill

Her first lesson in History starts at Bunker Hill in Boston. Helen climbed the monument here, counting the steps and wondered whether the soldiers too did the same and shot at the enemy on the ground.

Helen's First Trip on Sea Voyage

One day, Helen went to Plymouth. This was her first trip on ocean and the first voyage in steamboat. She takes keen interest in the great rock on which the pilgrims (from England) landed in 1620. She feels proud of the great brave men who fought for America's Independence.

हेलेन की बोस्टन यात्रा

मई, 1888 में Helen (हेलेन) की Boston (बोस्टन) यात्रा उसके लिए महत्त्वपूर्ण थी। इससे पहले भी हेलेन एक बार बाल्टमोर की ट्रेन यात्रा कर चुकी थी, परंतु यह यात्रा पिछली यात्रा से अलग थी इस यात्रा में उसकी माँ और शिक्षिका Miss Sullivan (मिस सुलिवान) भी साथ थीं।

नैंसी, हेलेन की गुड़िया का आकारहीन होना

जब वे बोस्टन पहुँचे, धोबिन ने Nancy (नैंसी) (हेलेन की गुड़िया) को, जो गंदी हो गई थी, नहला दिया, स्नान के बाद वह रूई के अवशेष की तरह निराकार हो गई और साथ ही उसकी दो आँखें ही बची थीं, जो हेलेन की तरफ निराशा से देख रही थीं।

बोस्टन शहर-एक परीलोक-सा

जब हेलेन बोस्टन शहर पहुँची, तो उसे ऐसा लगा जैसे कि सच में वह परीलोक में है। जैसे ही वे अंधों के लिए बने हुए Perkins Institute (परकिंस इंस्टीट्यूट) पहुँचे, हेलेन ने वहाँ दोस्त बनाए इस बात से हेलेन को बहुत खुशी हुई कि वहाँ पर सारे बच्चे उसी की शैली में ही बात कर रहे थे।

बंकर हिल का भ्रमण

उसके लिए इतिहास का प्रथम पाठ बोस्टन के Bunker Hill (बंकर हिल) के साथ शुरू हुआ। सीढ़ियों को गिनते हुए हेलेन ने Monument (स्मारक) की चढ़ाई की और उसने स्मारक पर चढ़ते हुए नीचे सीढ़ियों को गिना और वह सोच रही थी क्या सैनिक शत्रु पर गोली चलाने के लिए इतनी ऊँचाई पर चढ़े थे।

हेलेन की प्रथम समुद्री यात्रा

एक दिन हेलेन Plymouth (प्लॉयमाउथ) गई। यह महासागर की तथा Steamboat (स्टीमबोट) की उसकी पहली समुद्री यात्रा थी। एक The Great Rock (चट्टान) में हेलेन ने खास दिलचस्पी ली थी, जहाँ पर England (इंग्लैंड) से आए तीर्थयात्री 1620 में उतरे थे। उसने उन महान् साहसी योद्धाओं के लिए गर्व महसूस किया, जो America Independence (अमेरिका की स्वतंत्रता) के लिए लड़े थे।

Friendship with William Endicott and his Daughter

Helen had many pleasant memories of the time she spent in Mr Endicott's house. One day when she visited Mr Endicott's beautiful home at Beverly farms, she felt happy in the rose garden and was delighted to be greeted by their two dogs Leo and Fritz. Helen fed sugar to the horse Nimrod. Helen played with sand on the beach while Mr Endicott told her stories of the many ships that trailed from Boston to Europe. Helen found a good friend in Mr Endicott and thus called Boston "The City of Kind Hearts."

बिलियम एंडीकॉट और उनकी बेटियों से मित्रता

हेलेन के पास उस समय की बहुत-सी अच्छी यादें थीं, जो उसने Mr Endicott (मि एंडीकॉट) के घर पर बिताई थी। एक बार जब वह मि एंडीकॉट के Beverly Farms (बेवर्ले फार्म) वाले घर पर गई, तो उनके गुलाब के बगीचे और दो पालतू कुत्तों Leo and Fritz (लिओ और फ्रिट्ज) के अभिवादन की खुशी से अभिभूत हो गई। हेलेन ने उनके घोड़े Nimrod (निम्रोद) को चीनी खिलाई। जब हेलेन समुद्र के किनारे पर रेत से खेल रही थी, तब मि एंडीकॉट ने उसे उन बड़े जहाजों के बारे में बताया जो Europe (यूरोप) जाने के लिए बोस्टन से चलते थे। मि एंडीकॉट के रूप में हेलेन को एक अच्छा दोस्त मिला और इसलिए उसने इस शहर को "The City of Kind Hearts" (दयालु हृदय वाले लोगों का शहर) का नाम दिया।

Word Meaning

Departure	– प्रस्थान	Restless	– बेचैन
Excitable	– उमंगपूर्ण	Amused	– आश्चर्यचकित
Eager	– उत्सुक	Delicious	– स्वादिष्ट
Sunbonnet	– टोपी	Absorbed	– सोख लेना
Reproachfully	– निराशापूर्वक	Scarcely	– शायद ही
Appreciate	– प्रशंसा करना	Gathered	– जमा होना
Pleasure	– खुशी	Companionship	– भाईचारा
Convince	– राजी करना	Monument	– इमारत
Voyage	– समुद्री यात्रा	Rumble	– गर्जना
Pilgrims	– तीर्थयात्री	Toils	– कड़ी मेहनत
Imagination	– कल्पना	Splendour	– शानदार
Enterprise	– उद्यम	Idealised	– आदर्श बनाना
Generous	– उदार	Disappointed	– निराश
Shame	– शर्म	Glory	– महानता
Swiftest	– सबसे तेज	Lump	– एक बड़ा टुकड़ा

Important Questions

Questions based on the Plot of the Chapter

Q 1. Why does Helen say, 'I will not have occasion to refer to Nancy again'?

हेलेन ने ऐसा क्यों कहा, ''मैं नैंसी का दोबारा परिचय नहीं दे पाऊँगी''?

↳ बोस्टन यात्रा पर हेलेन के खिलौने का गंदा हो जाना – बोस्टन जाने पर खिलौने का धोबिन द्वारा साफ करना – धोने के बाद खिलौने का आकारहीन हो जाना – खिलौने में दो आँखें ही बची होना – खिलौना लगभग बेकार-सा हो जाना।

Ans. During the journey to Boston, Nancy got a bit of dirty. So, the laundress, on arriving Boston wanted to give Nancy a bath.
When Helen gave her the consent to do so she took Nancy to the bath and what came as a result was that Nancy seemed to be a clump and a mass of cotton only and no more a doll.
It got shapeless and weired too. Only the eyes in the form of two beads remained on the face of the doll.

Q 2. Helen has her first lesson in history at Bunker hill. Narrate her experience.

हेलेन का बंकर पहाड़ी से इतिहास का प्रथम पाठ लेने के अनुभव का वर्णन कीजिए।

↳ बोस्टन के परकिंस इंस्टीट्यूट से बाहर घूमने का कार्यक्रम बनना – बंकर हिल पर जाना – बंकर हिल से ही आजादी की लड़ाई लड़ी गई – हेलेन बंकर हिल की सीढ़ियों पर चढ़ी – हेलेन के द्वारा महसूस करना कि कैसे अमेरिकी सिपाहियों ने लड़ाई लड़ी होगी – इतिहास का प्रथम पाठ।

Ans. When Helen was staying at Boston then Perkins Institute arranged some outdoors for the children there. This outdoor was for Bunker hill, that was one of the most sought after monuments related to the freedom fight of America. It was the place from whose top the soldiers of America shot the millitants and helped America to get freedom. This was a great place.

When Helen reached there, she went to the top of Bunker hill by using the stairs and she counted it too. This was in order to know how the brave soldiers went to the top and how they fought. This was her first lesson in history.

Vacation at Brewster on Cape Cod

Before summer holidays, it was decided that Helen should spend her vacations at Brewster on Cape Cod which delighted Helen as she heard wonderful stories about the sea.

Helen's First Experience of Ocean

Helen had read about the ocean, but had not experienced one as she lived far inland. As soon as she came near the ocean, she in her bathing set dived into the cold water without any fear. The heavy waves of ocean pushed her from one side to another. Soon the sea threw Helen back on the shore where her teacher, Miss Sullivan grabbed her in her arms.

Miss Sullivan Gave Helen a Crab

On the shore, Miss Sullivan gave Helen a huge crab. Thinking that the crab would make a delightful pet, Helen caught it by the tail and put it in a trough near the well. Unfortunately, the crab came out by well the next morning and disappeared into its natural environment.

Word Meaning

Vivid	– रंग–बिरंगा	Whiff	– खुशबू
Intense	– सशक्त	Longing	– इच्छा
Mighty	– ताकतवर	Roar	– गर्जना
Leaped	– उछल–कूद करना	Plunged	– छलांग लगाना
Billows	– सशक्त लहरें	Buoyant	– तैरना
Exquisite	– बेहतरीन	Quivering	– काँपते हुए
Ecstasy	– खुशी	Thrust	– अचानक धकेलना
Frantic	– बेकार	Frolic	– खुशी–खुशी

गर्मी की छुट्टियाँ केप कॉड के ब्रूस्टर में

Summer Vacation (गर्मी की छुट्टियाँ) पड़ने से पहले तय हुआ कि हेलेन अपनी छुट्टियाँ Cape Cod (केप कॉड) के Brewster (ब्रूस्टर) में बिताएगी, जिससे Helen (हेलेन) को काफी प्रसन्नता हुई थी, क्योंकि उसने समुद्र के बारे में बहुत-सी कहानियाँ सुन रखी थीं।

हेलेन का समुद्र का पहला अनुभव

हेलेन ने समुद्र के बारे में पढ़ा था, परंतु उसे अनुभव नहीं था, क्योंकि वह मैदानी हिस्से की निवासी थी। जैसे ही वह समुद्र के पास आई, वैसे ही वह बिना डरे समुद्र के ठंडे पानी में कूद पड़ी। समुद्र की तेज लहरें उसे एक तरफ से दूसरी तरफ खींच रही थीं। जल्द ही एक लहर ने उसे किनारे पर ला दिया, जहाँ उसकी शिक्षिका Miss Sullivan (मिस सुलिवान) ने उसे अपनी बाँहों में पकड़ा।

मिस सुलिवान ने एक केकड़ा हेलेन को दिया

समुद्र के किनारे से मिस सुलिवान ने हेलेन को एक बड़ा Crab (केकड़ा) दिया। हेलेन ने यह सोचकर कि केकड़ा एक पालतू पशु होगा, हेलेन ने उसकी पूँछ पकड़कर उसे कुएँ के पास एक गर्त में डाल दिया। दुर्भाग्यवश, अगली सुबह केकड़ा कुएँ से बाहर आया और अपने प्राकृतिक वातावरण में गायब हो गया।

Clasped	– पकड़ लेना	Tender	– कोमल
Embrace	– गले लगाना	Recovered	– वापस आना
Panic	– घबराहट	Pebbles	– कंकड़
Rattling	– खड़खड़ाना	Ponderous	– वजनदार
Racked	– तह लगाना	Terrific	– भयावह
Tang	– जोरदार	Untainted	– बिना क्षति के
Trough	– पानी रखने का बर्तन	Disappointment	– निराशा

Important Questions

Questions based on the Plot of the Chapter

Q 1. Why is Helen excited about her summer vacations at Brewster on Cape Cod?

केप कॉड में अपनी गर्मी की छुट्टियाँ बिताने के लिए हेलेन ज्यादा उत्सुक क्यों थी?

परकिंस इंस्टीट्यूट में गर्मी की छुट्टियाँ पड़ना – हेलेन का मिस सुलिवान के साथ केप कॉड समुद्र देखने के लिए जाना – हेलेन का कभी समुद्र नहीं देखना – मिस सुलिवान का हेलेन को समुद्र के बारे में पढ़ाना – हेलेन का बहुत ही उत्सुक होना।

Ans. It was the time for the summer vacations at Perkins Institute. But just before the vacation to come it was decided that Helen should stay with Miss Sullivan and they should go to Cape Cod at Brewster where there is a great sea that awaits for them. Helen was much excited about all this. It was because of the fact that she had heard about the beauty and magnificence of the sea, but she had never been there and when she had a great chance to go there her excitements have got no end at all.

Company of Miss Sullivan was another thing that had added to the excitement. Another reason for this excitement was the availability of friends there. All the kids were used to the language of Helen and she felt the amiability in their company. Therefore, Helen was too much excited to be in the Cape Cod during her summer vacations.

Q 2. How does the sea plunges Helen into the water?

हेलेन को समुद्र के पानी में कैसे फेंका गया?

हेलेन में समुद्र देखने की प्रबल इच्छा होना – हेलेन का समुद्र के किनारे पहुँचना – हेलेन का समुद्र में छलांग लगा देना – लहरों के द्वारा इधर-उधर फेंका जाना – हेलेन का मदद के लिए चिल्लाना – अंततः मिस सुलिवान द्वारा बचाया जाना।

Ans. Helen's curiosity and her excitement about the visit of sea had no endings at all. It had deeply influenced her and it had a great impact on her mind that one can say that she was gripped in it. She could not control her emotions when she reached the shore and in the same influence she dived in water. As she dived, so did the sea reply and then she was being tossed up and down all the way.

She was crying for help, but none came to rescue her. She was being thrown every where in the deep sea. Finally, a strong sea wave brought her near the shore where she was able to grip Miss Sullivan at last.

All that happened because of the mental uproar that Helen had in her mind from her childhood and it was because she had been listening about the sea, but didn't get a chance to be there ever in her whole life. And when she did she got the outburst of the sea.

Q 3. The crab might make a delightful pet, according to Helen. Narrate her experience with the crab.

हेलेन के केकड़े से जुड़े अनुभव का वर्णन करें।

मिस सुलिवान द्वारा एक केकड़े को पकड़ना – हेलेन को मिस सुलिवान द्वारा केकड़े का मिलना – हेलेन का केकड़े पालने का निर्णय लेना – हेलेन द्वारा केकड़े को घर लाना – केकड़े को पानी के टब में रख देना – अगले दिन सुबह केकड़े का वहाँ से गायब हो जाना – हेलेन को केकड़े के गायब होने का दुःख होना।

Ans. When Helen was on the seashore with her teacher Miss Sullivan there was plenty of joy came through Helen's way. The exciting event took place when Helen was given a crab by Miss Sullivan. Helen immediately thought that she would keep this crab as a pet in her house.

She alongwith Miss Sullivan brought that pet. She decided to keep that crab in a water trough near about well so that a similar habitat could be established for the crab.

When in the next morning, she came to see the crab in that trough she found that it was gone. Helen felt very much disappointed by that. But she later realised that the crab was good in its natural habitat and became happy afterwards.

This experience let her know that home of someone should not be disturbed as it gives the desired peace. Moreover, the creature was so maniac about his dwelling place that he went after it ever when it was far from the house.

Question Digest

Term I

Questions based on the Plot

Q 1. Why does Helen consider the old fashioned garden the paradise of her childhood?

हेलेन अपने पुराने बगीचे को अपने बचपन का स्वर्ग क्यों मानती है?

Ans. The house where Helen lived was completely covered with vines, climbing roses and honeysuckle. It looked like an arbour and the little porch was hidden from view by a screen of yellow roses and smilax. The house and the surrounding trees and fences were covered with beautiful English ivy.

Its old fashioned garden was the paradise of Helen's childhood, because even before her teacher came, she used to feel along the square stiff boxwood hedges and guided by the smell, would find the first violets and lilies when she lost her temper.

She went to find comfort and hid her hot face in the cool leaves and grass. It was a joy for her to lose herself in this garden of flowers, to wander happily from spot to spot and then suddenly to come upon a beautiful wine, which she recognised by its leaves and blossoms and knew it was the wine which covered the tumble – down summer house at the other end of the garden. Here also were trailing clematis, dropping jasmine and some rare sweet flowers called butterfly lilies, because their fragile wings resembled butterfly wings.

The roses were the loveliest of all. She had never found in the green houses of the North such heart – satisfying roses as the climbing roses of the southern home.

They used to hang in ling festoons from her porch, filling the whole air with their fragrance, untainted by any earthy smell and in the early morning, washed in the dew, they felt so soft, so pure and Helen could not help wondering if they did not help wondering if they did not resemble the asphodels of the god's garden.

Q 2. Who were Helen's constant companions? How did she spend time with them?

हेलेन के साथी कौन थे? वह उनके साथ समय कैसे व्यतीत करती थी?

Ans. Helen was closest to Martha Washington, the daughter of their cook and Belle, an old setter and a great hunter when she was younger. They were her constant companions. Martha understood Helen's sign language and she seldom had any difficulty in making Martha do as she wished. It pleased Helen to domineer over her and Martha generally submitted to her tyranny rather than risk a hand – to – hand fight. Helen had her own way most of the time. Both Helen and Martha spent a great deal of time in the kitchen kneading dough balls, helping in making ice- cream and grinding coffee, quarrelling over the cake bowl and feeding the hens and turkey that swarmed around the kitchen steps.

Many of them were so tame that they ate from Helen's hand. They sat on the pile of woods and the cook had roasted the cake. Martha and Helen would go to egg hunting in the long grass. But Helen always insisted that she would carry the eggs home as Martha might drop the eggs. They also went to the shed where the corn was stored, the stable where the horses were kept and the yard where the cows were milked, morning and evening. Before Christmas, as Helen and Martha enjoyed the pleasant odours of the cakes and the pies being baked, they were given the titbits so that they would keep quite. They were allowed to grind the spices, pick over the raisins and lick the stirring spoon.

Q 3. Why were Helen's parents deeply grieved and perplexed? How did this grief finally lessen?

हेलेन के माता-पिता दुःखी और चिंतित क्यों थें? यह चिंता कैसे समाप्त हुई?

Ans. As Helen's desire to herself grew, she realised that the few signs which she has learnt to communicate with others were becoming inadequate. Not being able to make others around her and understand her, Helen got thoroughly frustrated and struggled to free herself. She finally broke down in tears, got exhausted and soon these outbursts happened frequently - sometimes every hour. Helen's helplessness disturbed her parents and made them anxious since they lived a long way from any school for the deaf or the blind and it seemed unlikely that anyone would come to

Tuscumbia to teach a child who was both deaf and dumb. This further perplexed her parents. Also Helen's relatives and friends doubted whether Helen could be taught.

Helen's mother's only ray of hope was from Dickens' "American Notes". She had read his account of Laura Bridgman and remembered vaguely that she was deaf and blind, yet had been educated. When Helen was about six years old, Mr Keller, Helen's father had heard of an oculist in Baltimore, who had been successful in many cases that seemed hopeful. So, her parents at once decide to take Helen to Baltimore to visit this doctor to see if anything could be done for Helen's eyes.

At Baltimore, Dr Chisholm who was specialised in diseases and disorders of the eyes. He was not able to do anything for Helen but suggested that she could be educated and advised Mr Keller to consult Dr Graham Bell who would be able to give him information about schools and teachers of deaf and blind children.

Q 4. How did Miss Sullivan teach Helen to spell words into her hand ?

मिस सुलिवान ने हेलेन को शब्दों का उच्चारण करना कैसे सिखाया?

Ans. The morning after Helen's teacher came, she went into her room and gave her a doll. The blind children at the Perkins Institution had sent it and Laura Bridgman had dressed it. After Helen played with the doll for a while, Miss Sullivan slowly spelt into her hand the word, "d-o-l-l". Helen found this finger play interesting and tried to imitate it. When she succeeded in making the letters correctly, she ran to her mother, heldup her hand and made the letters for doll. In the days that followed, Helen learnt many more new words like pin, hat, cup, sit, stand and walk. However, it took some weeks but Helen understood that everything had a name.

Q 5. Narrate the experience Helen had with nature which taught her that 'nature is not always kind'?

हेलेन के उस अनुभव का वर्णन कीजिए, जिससे यह साबित होता है कि प्रकृति हमेशा उदार नहीं होती है।

Ans. Helen loved nature especially the flowers, the birds ,the trees and the butterflies and when she lost her temper, she liked being among nature. She found it comforting to be amongst the flowers and the leaves.

She also learnt how plants grew from the sun and the rain. However, one unfortunate experience taught her that nature is not always kind.

One day, Miss Sullivan and Helen were returning from a walk. The day became warm and sultry so they stopped a couple of times under trees for short rests. The last halt was under a cherry tree, a short distance from the house. As the tree was easy to climb, Helen with Miss Sullivan's assistance scrambled to a seat in the branches. It was so cool up in the tree that Miss Sullivan proposed that they would eat their lunch there. She then left Helen, who promised to keep still, till her teacher went to home to fetch the lunch.

Q 6. How did Miss Sullivan teach Helen the meaning of the word, 'love'?

मिस सुलिवान ने हेलेन को 'प्यार' शब्द का अर्थ कैसे समझाया?

Ans. One morning Helen found a few early violets in the garden and brought them to Miss Sullivan who gave her a kiss. Since, Helen only liked her mother to kiss her, Miss Sullivan put her arm gently round her and spelled into her hand, "I love Helen". This was the first time, Helen asked her teacher the meaning of love.

Miss Sullivan drew her closer and was pointing to her heart saying that love was there. Helen was puzzled as she could not understand anything unless she touched it. She curiously enquired whether the sweetness of the violets was love and the warmth of the sun was love. Each time her teacher exclaimed that neither of the two were the meaning of love. One day when it rained slightly, Helen again asked whether this was love. Finally, her teacher found a suitable explanation and said that love was something like the clouds that were in the sky before the sun came out. "You can never touch the clouds, but you can feel the rain and you know how glad the flowers and thirsty earth feels after a hot day." Similarly, she explained that love could not be touched, but one could feel the sweetness that it poured into everything. Without love you would not be happy or want to play.

Q 7. Helen read and studied outdoor. Narrate her experience with the natural surroundings.

हेलेन को बाहर अध्ययन करना पसंद था। प्राकृतिक वातावरण से जुड़े उसके अनुभव का वर्णन करें।

Ans. Helen and Miss Sullivan read and studied outdoor, preferring the sunlit woods to the house. All her early lessons had in them the breath of woods- the fine resinous odour of the pine needles, blended with the perfume of wild grapes. Seated in the gracious shade of the wild tulip tree, Helen learnt that everything had a lesson and a suggestion. The loveliness of things taught Helen their use. Everything that could hum, or buzz, or sing or bloom had a part in her education – noisy-throated frogs, katydids and crickets which she held in her hand, little downy chickens and wild flowers, the dogwood blossoms, meadow violets and budding fruit trees. She felt the bursting cotton bolls and felt their soft fibre and fuzzy seeds; she felt the low soughing of the wind through the cornstalks, the silky rustling of the long leaves and the snort of the pony in the pastures.

At times in the early morning, Helen went to the garden while the heavy dew lay on the grass and flowers, felt the soft rose petals or the beautiful lilies as they swayed in the morning breeze.

Another favourite haunt of Helen's was the orchard, where the fruit ripened early in July. The large downy peaches would reach her hands and as the joyous breeze flew about the trees, the apples tumbled at Helen's feet.

Q 8. What happened to the canary which Miss Sullivan presented Helen on Christmas ?

मिस सुलिवान ने हेलेन को जो गाने वाली चिड़िया दी थी, उस चिड़िया का क्या हुआ?

Ans. When Miss Sullivan presented Helen a canary, a singing bird, Helen was full of happiness. She named him Tim and he was so tame that he hopped on her finger and ate candied cherries out of her hand. Miss Sullivan taught her to take all the care of her new pet. Helen prepared his bath every morning after breakfast, made his cage clean and sweet, filled his cups with fresh seed and water from the well-house and hung a piece of chickweed in his swing.

One morning Helen left the cage on the window-seat while she went to fetch water for his bath. When she returned, Helen felt a big cat brush past her as she opened the door. When she put her hand in the cage, Helen could not feel Tim's wings or his tiny claws. She soon realised that the cat had eaten Tim and that she would never again meet her sweet little singer. This made her extremely sad.

Q 9. Narrate Helen's experience at the Perkins Institution for the blind.

परकिंस इंस्टीट्यूट से जुड़े हेलेन के अनुभव का वर्णन कीजिए।

Ans. Helen and her teacher, Miss Sullivan reached Boston and scarcely had they arrived at the Perkins Institution for the blind when Helen began to make friends with the little blind children. It delighted her immensely that they knew the manual alphabet. It was a joy to be able to talk with other children in her own language. Till now, she had been like a foreigner speaking through an interpreter. However, Helen was aware that the children who happily played with her and who could read books with their fingers were blind, but not deaf.

Helen felt that since they could hear, they must have a sort of "second sight'. They were so happy and contented that Helen lost all sense of pain in the pleasure of their companionship.

One day spent with the blind children made Helen feel thoroughly at home in her new environment, and she looked eagerly from one pleasant experience to another as the days flew swiftly by.

Q 10. What made Helen realise that it is not wise to force animals out of their natural surroundings ?

हेलेन को कब अहसास हुआ कि जानवरों को उनके आवास से अप्राकृतिक रूप से विस्थापित करना सही नहीं हैं?

Ans. While vacationing at Brewster at Cape Cod near the sea, one day Miss Sullivan attracted Helen's attention to a great horseshoe crab, the first one she had ever seen. It suddenly occurred to Helen that he might be a delightful pet, so she seized him by its tail with both hands and carried him home. This feat pleased Helen highly as his body was very heavy and it took all her strength to drag him half a mile.

She pleaded with Miss Sullivan to put the crab in a trough near the well where Helen was confident that he would be secure. But the next morning, when Helen went to the trough, the crab had disappeared. Nobody knew, where he had gone or how he had escaped. Helen was disappointed, but slowly came to realise that it was not kind or wise to force animals out of their natural environment. This thought made her feel better and happy.

Q 11. Narrate the incident when Helen, her sister and her teacher missed getting hit by a train.

उस घटना का वर्णन कीजिए जब हेलेन, मिस सुलिवान और मिल्ट्रेड ट्रेन से टकराते-टकराते बच गए थे।

Ans. Helen spent the autumn months with her family on a mountain called Fern Quarry. One day Helen, Mildred and Miss Sullivan were lost in the woods and wandered for hours trying to find a path to their house. Suddenly, Mildred pointed to the trestle which spanned a deep gorge. It was very difficult to walk over as the ties were wide apart and as narrow as knives. Since, it was late and it growing dark, the trestle was a short-cut to their house, so they started to walk over it. Helen had to feel for the rails with her toe but she was not afraid.

All of a sudden, a train was heard at a distance and Mildred cautioned them. In the next minute, the train would have been upon them if they had not climbed down upon the crossbraces while the train rushed over their heads.

Q 12. Helen experiences the treasures of the snow on her visit to a New Englang village. Describe her experience.

न्यू इंग्लैंड के एक गाँव में हेलेन ने बर्फ के खजाने को महसूस किया। उसके इस अनुभव का वर्णन कीजिए।

Ans. One winter Helen visited a village in New England with its frozen lakes and vast snow fields. The trees and bushes had stripped off their leaves and birds had flown away leaving their empty nests behind. All lives seemed to have come to a standstill and even when the sun shone, the day was shrunk and cold. One day there was a snowstorm which lasted for three days. Snow flakes rushed here and there furiously.Helen and the others sat around a great fire and told merry tales and frolicked and forgot that they were in the midst of deserted and isolated place, shut in from all communication with the outside world. During the night, the fury of the wind increased and the rafters creaked and strained, and the branches from the trees rattled and beat against the windows. Once the storm ended on the third day, the sun broke out and heaps of ice with fallen leaves and branches were found all over. When the rays of the sun fell upon the bare trees, the twigs sparkled like diamonds. Before the ice could completely melt, there was another snow storm and Helen hardly got the chance to feel the earth under her feet all winter.

Q 13. How does Helen learn to speak in the spring of 1890 ?

सन् 1890 मे हेलेन ने बसंत ऋतु मे कैसे बोलना सीखा।

Ans. The impulse to speak had always been strong within Helen. She used to make noises, keeping one hand on her throat while the other hand felt the movement of her lips. She was pleased with anything that made a noise, and liked to feel the cat purr and the dog bark. She also liked to keep her hand on a singer's throat, or on a piano when it was being played. She used to feel the motion of her mother's lips and craved to move her own lips too to produce sound, but she was unable to do so.

Helen was entirely dependent on the manual alphabet which created a gap in her life. She felt limited while communicating with other people and a sense of narrowness gripped her. This feeling began to agitate her violently and she persisted in using her lips and voice. Her friends feared that Helen might not be able to learn and to speak and this disability would lead to disappointment.Helen however persisted to speak and in the meanwhile she heard the story of Ragnhild Kaata,a deaf and blind girl in Norway who had actually been taught to speak.In 1890, Mrs Lamson returned from Norway and as she told Helen the success story of Ragnhild, she was filled with a keen desire and eagerness to learn and to speak. Helen was not satisfied till her teacher took her to Miss Sarah Fuller, principal of the Horace Mann School. This lovely, sweet-natured lady offered to teach Helen herself and the lessons began from the 26th of March, 1890.

Mrs Fuller's method was this—she passed Helen's hand lightly over her face, and let her feel the position of her tongue and lips when she made a sound.

Questions based on the Character-Sketch

Q 14. What were the special qualities in Helen which made her "the greatest woman of our age"?

हेलेन के उन गुणों का वर्णन कीजिए जो उसे 'एक महान महिला' बनाते हैं।

Ans. Helen Adams Keller was born on June 27th, 1880 in Tuscumbia, Albama to Kate and Arthur H Keller. She lost her eye sight and hearing after an illness when she was nineteen months old. Although, her disability left her shattered, she achieved a lot in life with her will power, dedication and focus. She understood the need for education and was the first deaf and blind person to earn a Bachelor of Arts degree.

She did not want to depend on others most of the time -even before her teacher came. Helen used to spend her time in the garden and feel the flowers and plants to comfort herself. Again later in life, when Helen started reading books, she preferred doing it on her own than have Miss Sullivan read and re-read the stories. Since her childhood, Helen was curious to learn and know about the things around her so she felt every object and observed every motion. To communicate with others, she initially learnt some signs which were crude, but as the time passed, she developed refined skills to talk to the other people. When she was accused of plagiarism, she felt disgraced, but over a period of time, she put this incident behind and started to write again.

This showed her courageous side. Physically too, she was brave and daring when she climbed a tree on her own inspite of the earlier cherry tree incident and at Fern Quarry. She again displayed her strength when she walked on the narrow trestle without fear.

She travelled with her teacher to various places and learned about these places, the natural surroundings, the sea, the mountains and the rivers. In a fun way, she got to learn geography and history.

Q 15. Give a character sketch of Helen's father, Arthur H. Keller.

हेलेन के पिता आर्थर केलर का चरित्र-चित्रण कीजिए।

Ans. Helen's father Arthur H Keller was a captain in the Confederate Army and was the editor of a newspaper. Helen describes her father as the most loving and indulgent person who was devoted to his family. His other passion was hunting. He was a great hunter and he also loved his gun. He was very fond of dogs and the Keller family had a couple of dogs as pets. He enjoyed having guests over to their house and entertained them well.

He liked gardening and took special pride in his huge garden which was full of beautiful flowers, bushes and trees. He raised the finest watermelons and strawberries and used to bring the first ripe grapes and juiciest berries for Helen. Since, Helen liked nature, Mr Keller held her little hands and led her from tree to tree, from vine to vine and his eager delight in whatever pleased her.

He was a famous storyteller and after Helen acquired language, he used to spell clumsily into her hand his cleverest anecdotes, even repeat them at times. When doctors had to be contacted for Helen, he was hopeful and got in touch with them as soon as he could.

Helen was in the North when her father died of an illness in 1896 and his passing away was her first ever experience with death and her first great sorrow.

Q 16. Give a character sketch of Miss Anne Sullivan highlighting the qualities she had in her which made Helen the person she was.

मिस सुलिवान के व्यक्तिगत गुणों का चरित्र-चित्रण करें और यह भी दिखाएँ कि हेलेन के विकास में उनका कितना अहम योगदान था।

Ans. Miss Anne Sullivan was sent to teach Helen who was deaf and blind and as a teacher she was extremely patient and tolerant with Helen. She knew the problems, a child without seeing and hearing must be facing and was aware of the psychology of such a person. She handled sensitively, but firmly when Helen got frustrated and threw tantrums and dealt with each incident in a practical way. She knew what Helen wanted and accordingly taught her to communicate with the people around her.

Miss Sullivan made Helen confident by making her selfdependent. She took her to various places and taught her in the natural surroundings, encouraging Helen to touch, feel and explore. She motivated Helen to read, write and also speak like others.
A teacher like her was not only the guiding force for Helen, but a true friend, companion and a mother-like figure.

As she accompanied Helen on her visits to the doctor to places away from their home and to school and college, she had to be aquainted with the education and teaching methods so she worked very hard at learning herself and then imparting the same to Helen. Miss Sullivan's selfless nature, dedication and perseverance matched with Helen's eagerness to learn, became the reason for Helen's achievements.

From the beginning of Helen's education, Miss Sullivan made it a practice to speak to Helen as she would be a hearing child. She did not underestimate Helen which was very important for a teacher to understand. It was Miss Sullivan who unfolded and developed the knowledge about life in Helen.

Helen appreciates the fact that her teacher's genius, her quick sympathy, her loving tact made the early years of her education so beautiful. Miss Sullivan seized the right moment to impart knowledge that made it so pleasant and acceptable to Helen. She realised that a child's mind is like a shallow brook which ripples and dances merrily over the stony course of its education. All her best wisdom was due to Miss Sullivan. Without her teacher, Helen would be lost in her dark and silent world.

Miss Sullivan became Helen's eyes and ears, but finally due to her constant support, trust and motivation, Helen could study and learn like other students and could write and speak too. Miss Sullivan did not give up easily and when Helen was accused of plagiarism, her constant motivation and spirited nature helped Helen to come out of the fear of writing.

Q 17. Give a character sketch of Helen's mother, Kate Adams Keller.

हेलेन की माँ, केट एडम्स केलर का चरित्र-चित्रण कीजिए।

Ans. Kate Adams Keller was Arthur Keller's second wife and much younger to him. She was tall, fair complexioned with pretty blue eyes. She was a loving and caring mother and did whatever was best for her children. Intelligent and widely read it was Kate Keller who read Dickens's "American Notes" and came to know about Laura Bridgman who inspite of being deaf and blind, had been educated.

She had a keen memory which made her remember that Dr Howe who had discovered the way to teach the deaf and blind, had been dead many years. She encouraged Helen's father to take her to Baltimore to visit an eminent oculist.

This shows that Kate did not give up hope easily. Anxious for her daughter, to be guided by a trained teacher, she welcomes Miss Sullivan and respects the idea of giving her liberty to take care of Helen in her own practical way.

She did not interfere in the teacher's methods of training and teaching which was very important in the initial phases of such a challenging education. She valued the effort, Miss Sullivan was putting in her daughter's training and when Helen returns after his speech training, Kate is speechless and as she hugs Helen, she was in tears with delight.

Nothing was as important for her than Helen's achievements. The knowledge that Helen could speak filled her with immense pleasure and joy. Kate's positive attitude and supportive and understanding nature allowed her to take up the difficult challenges which she had to face in life especially after the death of her husband.

She was a courageous lady who patiently dealt with a sensitive child like Helen and helped her overcome her disabilities. Her devotion to the family and undying spirit were a pillar of strength for the entire household.

Term II

Helen Recalls Her Experiences

In the autumn season Helen returns home and is happy that she has learnt new things about the world during her visit to the North of the country. She was always keen to discover new places and things around her. She spends the autumn months with her family at Fern Quarry, 14 miles from Tuscumbia.

हेलेन का अपने अनुभवों को याद करना

Autumn (पतझड़) के मौसम में Helen (हेलेन) वापस अपने घर आ गई और वह इस बात से खुश थी की उसने North (उत्तरी) क्षेत्र के बारे में बहुत सारी जानकारियाँ प्राप्त की थीं। वह हमेशा अपने आसपास नई जगह की और नई चीजों की खोज करने के लिए उत्सुक रहती थी। पतझड़ का पूरा महीना हेलेन ने अपने परिवार के साथ Fern Quarry (फर्न क्वैरी) नामक जगह पर बिताया, जो Tuscumbia (टुसकुंबिया) से 14 मील दूर था।

Helen Face the Train

At the foot of the mountains there was a railroad. One day Helen, Miss Sullivan and Mildred went down till there and wandered for hours without finding a path. They went along the rail tracks and on seeing a train coming suddenly, they climbed down upon the cross braces. Helen could feel the hot smoke upon her face. They finally reached home only to realise that the family was out looking for them.

हेलेन का ट्रेन से सामना होना

पहाड़ी के बिल्कुल निचले हिस्से में एक रेलवे लाइन थी। एक दिन Helen (हेलेन), Miss Sullivan (मिस सुलिवान) और Mildred (मिल्ड्रेड) तीनों घूमने के लिए वहाँ पर गए और घंटों तक वहाँ घूमते रहे और अंत में रास्ता भटक गए और रेल की पटरियों के साथ-साथ चलने लगे। सामने से एक ट्रेन आते देख वे तिरछी बंधनियों को पकड़कर नीचे उतर गए। हेलेन धुएँ और राख को अपने चेहरे के ऊपर महसूस कर सकती थी। अंतत: जब वे लोग वहाँ से घर पहुँचे, तो उन्होंने देखा कि परिवार के सभी लोग उन्हें ही खोजने गए हुए है।

Word Meaning

Recall	– याद करना	Cluster	– जमा होना
Treasures	– खजाना	Sympathy	– सहानुभूति
Behold	– देखना	Miracle	– चमत्कार
Quarry	– खुली जगह	Abandoned	– मना किया जाना
Frolicsome	– जीवंत	Bar	– रोकना
Splendid	– शानदार	Evergreen	– हरियाली

Important Questions

Questions based on the Plot of the Chapter

Q 1. Why did Helen's family go out to look for her, Mildred and Miss Sullivan? Narrate the experience.

हेलेन का परिवार हेलेन, मिल्ड्रेड और मिस सुलिवान को खोजने क्यों गया? उस अनुभव का वर्णन कीजिए।

फर्न क्वैरी में हेलेन, मिल्ड्रेड और मिस सुलिवान का एक साथ रहना – तीनों का जंगल में घूमना – घूमते हुए पहाड़ी के नीचे जाना – तीनों का वहाँ से रास्ता भूल जाना – घंटों भटकने के बाद शाम को घर आना – घर आने पर मालूम होना कि परिवार के लोगो का उन्हें खोजना।

Ans. While having a stay in Fern Quarry, Helen got a habit of walking in the forests of Fern Quarry alongwith Miss Sullivan and Mildred (her cousin). They used to go in search of wild fruits like persimmons and walnuts.

It was the favourite rambling of theirs and they would never miss a chance of it. One day they all went down hill where a railroad was being plyed. They wandered there for long and missed their path. They finally found it after a very long time in the evening.

It is therefore very obvious that they would have reached their home late. That's why the family went out in search of them.

12

Helen Visits a Village in New England

Ever since her first visit to Boston, Helen spent almost every winter in the North. Once on a visit to a New England village, Helen experienced and enjoyed the treasures of the snow. The trees were stripped off their leaves; birds had flown away leaving their empty nests.

The Snow Storm Lasted Three Days

One day the air became very chilly and then a snow storm lasting three days changed the look of the entire place. Snow flakes dropped silently.

In the evening a wind from the northeast grow up, and the snow flakes rushed here and there. Helen and others sat inside around a fire and told merry tales. The beams on the roof creaked and the strong winds turned everything upside down. After the storm stopped on the third day, the sun shone, but everything lay in heaps on the roads.

Tobogganing - Their Favourite Amusement

Tobogganing was everyone's favourite amusement. This winter sport requires snow and a carriage on which one sits. A boy would give a hard push and the toboggan would go sliding down the icy slopes. This was a great joy and also exhilarating.

हेलेन का न्यू इंग्लैंड के एक गाँव में भ्रमण

Boston (बोस्टन) की पहली यात्रा के बाद Helen (हेलेन) अपनी सारी सर्दियाँ उत्तरी हिस्से में बिताती थी। एक बार हेलेन New England (न्यू इंग्लैंड) के एक गाँव गई, वहाँ पर हेलेन ने बर्फ का खजाने के रूप में अनुभव किया। पेड़ के सारे पत्ते झड़ गए थे और चिड़ियाएँ भी अपने घोसलों को खाली करके उड़ चुकी थीं।

तीन दिन लगातार बर्फबारी का पड़ना

एक दिन चारों तरफ सर्द हवाएँ चल रही थीं, लगातार तीन दिनों तक बर्फीले तूफान का प्रकोप बना रहा, जिसने उस स्थान का दृश्य ही बदल दिया था। बर्फ के टुकड़े शांत होकर गिर रहे थे।

शाम के समय Northeast (उत्तर-पूर्व) दिशा की ओर से हवा बढ़ रही थी और बर्फ के लच्छे इधर-उधर उड़ रहे थे। हेलेन और अन्य लोग आग के आसपास बैठ गए और वहाँ कहानियों को सुनाया जा रहा था। उनकी छत की कड़िया चरमराने लगी तथा तेज व सर्द हवाओं ने सब कुछ तहस-नहस कर दिया था। तीसरे दिन तूफान रुकने के बाद सूरज चमका और सड़कों पर सब कुछ ढेर में निहित हो गया।

टोबोगगैनिंग–सबसे रुचिकर खेल

Tobogganing (टोबोगगैनिंग) सबका पसंदीदा मनोरंजक खेल था। यह शीतकालीन खेल है, जिसमें लोग Carriage (गाड़ी) में बैठकर बर्फ के ऊपर से फिसलते हुए आगे बढ़ते हैं। एक लड़का उनको धक्का देता और वे ढाल से नीचे लुढ़क जाते थे। यह एक लंबी और बड़ी खुशी थी।

Word Meaning

Frozen	– जमा हुआ	Vast	– विस्तृत तौर से
Stripped	– हटा दिया जाना	Wrinkled	– मुरझाया हुआ
Benumbed	– मृतप्राय	Withdrawn	– वापस करना
Vein	– शिरा	Decrepitly	– पुराना होना
Withered	– भद्दा	Transformed	– परिवर्तन लाना
Snowstorm	– बर्फीला तूफान	Flakes	– टुकड़ा
Descending	– नीचे आना	Scarcely	– शायद ही
Landscape	– भू-दृश्य	Furious	– खतरनाक
Frolicked	– खुशीपूर्वक खेलना	Desolate	– सुनसान
Solitude	– शांति	Fury	– कहर

Important Questions

Questions based on the Plot of the Chapter

Q 1. Describe the snow storm which Helen experienced in New England.

न्यू इंग्लैंड में हेलेन ने जो बर्फीला तूफान देखा उसके अनुभव का वर्णन कीजिए।

↗ हेलेन का न्यू इंग्लैंड के एक गाँव में भ्रमण करना – बर्फबारी और सर्दी का पड़ना – लोगों का घर से बाहर निकलना मुश्किल होना – तीन दिनों तक लगातार बर्फबारी का निरन्तर रहना – इसके पश्चात् मजेदार खेल टोबोगगैनिंग की शुरूआत होना।

Ans. Helen was enjoying her winter in a village of New England. Since, it was the time of winter so there was snow all over. Strong and chilly wind blew all over there making it furious for the people even to get out of their houses. It was so long and it lasted for three days and the whole area was filled with snow. No landscape could be seen. The heaped snow offered a great sport to the people.

They started Tobogganing which is fun to sit in a carriage and being driven away. This all put up a very brilliant scene out there and it was all very exhilarating. She had never seen such a strong and chilly cold ever. She was thinking about the fury that people had to face whenever such things happened. The life seemed to beg its virtue and worth to come alive, but nothing happened.

Q 2. Tobogganing was Helen's and other people's favourite amusement. Why was it so thrilling?

टोबोगगैनिंग हेलेन और दूसरे लोगों का सबसे मनपसंद कार्य था। यह इतना रोमांचक क्यों था?

टोबोगगैनिंग एक लोकप्रिय मजेदार खेल – टोबोगगैनिंग खेल का लोगों के बीच में अत्यधिक प्रसिद्ध होना – मनोरंजन के साथ इस खेल को खेलना – खेल में लोगों के एक साथ होने की वजह से उन्हें एक सूत्र में बाँधना – सामाजिक खेल का होना – बच्चे तथा वयस्क के लिए अत्यधिक प्रिय खेल होना।

Ans. Tobogganing was one of the most loved and also exhilarating games to play. It was played in the winter season when there was snow all over the periphery. The game was equally entertaining to everybody. The reason of it being a favourite of all is that it unites the people with the same thread. The game was played as; the persons had to be seated in a carriage and then somebody pushed it on the surface. It was a great fun coming out of the snow that kept everyone bound. Since, this game had an attribute of social mobility so everybody loved it. Childern as well as the young and adults liked the game equally. No one could resist getting lost in the fun of the game.

Q 3. How did the narrator describe the rays of the sun that fell after the snow ceased to fall?

जब बर्फबारी बंद हो गई, तो कथाकार ने सूर्य की किरणों के बारे में क्या वर्णन दिया?

सर्दियों के समय गाँव में लगातार बर्फबारी का होना – तीन दिन तक लगातार बर्फबारी का पड़ना – लोगों के मन में धूप के प्रति लालसा जगना – धूप निकलने से बर्फ का पिघलना – किरणों की वजह से बर्फ का हीरे की भाँति चमक उठना।

Ans. The village had witnessed enormous amount of snow in the last three days. The extent was so much that the whole region was filled with it and one could not past it. Yet people enjoyed it to the fullest, but in a sense people were a bit disturbed with it and they wanted to see the rays of sun glowing through the territory. When it happened it was brilliant. Snow was sparkling like diamonds and the bare trees were penetrated by it making them look fruitless to an extent. The rays of sun came like an angel in that biting cold people were awaiting for it since long.

Helen Learned to Speak

The urge to utter audible words was always there in Helen's heart and finally in the spring of 1890, she learned to speak. She made noises keeping one hand on her throat and with the other hand she felt the movement of her lips. She liked to keep her hand on a singer's throat or on a piano when it was being played. Helen remembered how she sat on her mother's lap and kept her hands on her face to feel the lip movements, after she had lost her hearing and sight. She remembered the meaning of one word water, which she pronounced 'wa-wa'.

Miss Fuller— Teacher and Trainer of Helen

Miss Fuller, principal of the Horace Mann School for the deaf at Boston, offered to teach Helen, beginning 26th March, 1890. In an hour, Helen learnt the six elements of speech : M, P, A, S, T, I. Helen uttered her first sentence, "It is warm". After this training, Helen felt as if she had come out of bondage and felt more confident and free.

Helen's Work was Practice, Practice, Practice

Since Helen had learnt only the elements of speech, she was unable to speak audibly and Miss Fuller and Miss Sullivan were the ones who could really understand her. However, Helen practiced a lot and worked very hard at trying to speak as clearly as possible. She felt happy at the thought that now her little sister, Mildred would understand her.

Helen Returned Home

When she returned after her training at speech, to Tuscumbia, her whole family came to the station to welcome her. Helen's mother hugged her, Mildred held her hand kissed it and her father expressed pride and affection in a big silence. She is now extremely happy and confident.

हेलेन का बोलना सीखना

Helen (हेलेन) के मन में हमेशा से ही बोलने की एक प्रबल इच्छा थी और 1890 के Spring (बसंत) में जाकर अंतत: उसने बोलना सीख लिया। अपने गले पर एक हाथ रखकर पहले वह कुछ आवाज निकालती और फिर दूसरे हाथ को अपने होठों पर रखकर अपनी ही आवाज को महसूस करने की कोशिश करती। वह गायक के गले पर तथा Piano (पियानो) पर, जब वह बजाया जाता था, हाथ रखना पसंद करती थी। इतना ही नहीं, जब बीमारी की वजह से हेलेन की बोलने और सुनने की क्षमता चली गई थी, तो वह अपनी माँ की गोद में बैठकर उनके चेहरे पर हाथ रखकर होठों की प्रतिक्रिया को महसूस करती। हेलेन को वाटर शब्द का मतलब याद था, जिसे वह 'वा-वा' कहती थी।

मिस फुलर–हेलेन की शिक्षक और प्रशिक्षक

Miss Fuller (मिस फुलर) Horace Mann School (होरैस मैन स्कूल) की प्रिंसिपल थीं, जो बहरों के लिए Bolten (बोल्टन) में था, उन्होनें 26 मार्च, 1890 से हेलेन को पढ़ाना प्रारम्भ कर दिया था। एक घंटे में हेलेन ने छ: ध्वनियाँ M, P, A, S, T, I को सीख लिया। हेलेन ने अपना पहला वाक्य "It is warm" बोला था। इस प्रशिक्षण के बाद, हेलेन को ऐसा लगा जैसे उसे एक बहुत बड़े बंधन से छुटकारा मिल गया हो और उसने विश्वास और स्वतंत्रता महसूस की।

हेलेन का निरंतर अभ्यास करने का जुनून

हेलेन ने भाषा के मूल तत्त्वों को सीख लिया था, परंतु वह अभी Miss Sullivan (मिस सुलिवान) और Miss Fuller (मिस फुलर) को छोड़ किसी से भी ढंग से बात नहीं कर पाती थी। हालाँकि स्पष्ट बोलने की कोशिश में हेलेन ने अभ्यास और कठिन परिश्रम करना निरंतर रखा। उसे इस बात से काफी खुशी मिलती थी कि उसकी छोटी बहन Mildred (मिल्ड्रेड) अब उसकी बातों को समझ सकेगी।

हेलेन की घर वापसी

ट्रेनिंग पूरी होने के बाद जब हेलेन वापस Tuscumbia (टुसकुंबिया) लौट रही थी, तो उसका पूरा परिवार उसके स्वागत के लिए रेलवे स्टेशन आया था। हेलेन की माँ ने उसे गले लगाया और मिल्ड्रेड ने उसके हाथ को चूमा और उसके पिता ने एक बड़ी चुप्पी के साथ अपने गर्व और खुशी को व्यक्त किया। इन सबको देखकर हेलेन को बहुत खुशी मिली और उसका आत्मविश्वास बढ़ गया।

Word Meaning

Impulse	– तीव्र इच्छा		Audible	– सुना जा सकने वाला
Imperative	– आवश्यक		Entirely	– पूरी तरह
Restraint	– अवरोध करना		Agitate	– परेशान होना
Vexing	– चिंतित		Scarcely	– शायद ही
Eagerness	– उत्सुकता		Resolved	– निश्चय कर लेना
Imitate	– नकल करना		Stammering	– हकलाना
Earnestly	– गंभीरता से		Pierces	– भेद देना
Appreciate	– प्रशंसा करना		Interpretation	– वर्णन करना
Fluttered	– लड़खड़ाना		Articulate	– स्पष्ट रूप से कहना
Peculiar	– विचित्र		Contend	– प्रतियोगिता
Accomplished	– पूरा करना		Obstacle	– अवरोध
Despondent	– निराश होना		Anticipated	– उम्मीद करना
Astonished	– आश्चर्यचकित		Discarded	– त्याग देना
Trembling	– काँपते हुए		Affection	– लगाव होना
Prophecy	– पूर्वानुमान		Fulfilled	– पूरा हो जाना

Important Questions

Questions based on the Plot of the Chapter

Q 1. How did Miss Fuller teach and train Helen to learn speech?

मिस फुलर ने हेलेन को बोलने की कला कैसे सिखाई?

↗ हेलेन का बोलने व सीखने का साहसिक फैसला लेना – मिस फुलर का हेलेन की ट्रेनर बनना – मिस फुलर ने हेलेन से कहा कि वह अपने होठों और जुबान पर हाथ रखकर गति का अनुमान लगाए – हेलेन का लगातार प्रयास करना – मिस फुलर द्वारा हेलेन को बोलने की कला को सिखाना – कुछ दिनों में हेलेन द्वारा बोलने की कला सीख लेना।

Ans. When Helen desired to learn the speech, it was a very big decision as it would take a lot of energy and effort. Miss Fuller decided to teach Helen the art of speech herself. She had been doing this for a long time, but it was a bit tough for her. She started training for Helen. She would say to Helen to keep her fingers on her mouth while she was uttering a word. Apart from this, she would ask Helen to practice regularly.

Helen paid heed to her words and that came out very positively. Finally, Helen got to know the first few elements of sound and later on, she learnt it very well. It was not easy for Miss Fuller at all, but determination made it possible.

Miss Fuller was the master who taught Helen the art of language speaking. Miss Fuller did her best   to initiate the process of bringing out the potential of Helen and afterwards perfection came so naturally to her.

Q 2. Who was Ragnhild Katta? Did her story inspire Helen?

राहिल्ड काट्टा कौन थी? क्या उसकी कहानी से हेलेन प्रभावित हुई थी?

राहिल्ड काट्टा का मिस फुलर की शिष्या होना – काट्टा का भी शारीरिक रूप से हेलेन की तरह होना – मिस फुलर की वजह से काट्टा का भी बोलना सीख लेना – हेलेन द्वारा शुरूआत में सीखने में परेशानी होना – काट्टा की कहानी से प्रेरणा लेकर हेलेन द्वारा बोलना सीखना।

Ans. Katta was one of the students of Miss Fuller at her school. She was deaf and dumb like Helen. Helen told Miss Fuller that Katta too had a wish that she could know the art of speech.

Miss Fuller helped her in realising her dream. Initially, when Helen was trying to learn the art of speech, it was difficult to her then the story of Katta came into play and she learnt that despite utmost difficulties, if Katta could learn this art, she could also do that .

This story was so motivating that it kept Helen going on the path of her wish to learn how to speak.

Katta was like a spark that ignited mental determination of Helen to learn language. Katta's extreme hard work was enough for Helen's wish to come to the forefront. She believed in her ability and thought if Katta could do it, then she too could do it. That was the motivation that Helen received from Katta's real life story of success.

Q 3. Who was Mrs Lamson? What did she tell to Helen?

श्रीमती लैमसन कौन थीं? हेलेन से उन्होंने क्या कहा?

➤ श्रीमती लैमसन का लाउरा ब्रिजमैन की शिक्षिका होना – उनके द्वारा स्वीडन और नॉर्वे का दौरा करना – हेलेन से मिलने आना – हेलेन की समस्या सुनना – राहिल्ड काट्टा की कहानी सुनाना – हेलेन का कहानी से प्रभावित होना – हेलेन द्वारा बोलने का फैसला लेना।

Ans. Mrs Lamson was one of the teachers of Laura Bridgman and she had just returned from her visit to Norway and Sweden. She came to meet Helen with a purpose.

When she met Helen, she came to know that Helen wanted to learn the art of speaking, but she was finding it difficult to learn. At that very moment, Mrs Lamson came up with the story of Katta, that story was so special to Helen and it inspired her completely.

The motivation led Helen towards the learning of a much needed art that changed the course of her life. Mrs Lamson stroy telling of Ragnhild Katta impressed Helen so much that her determination became very strong and she decided to repeat the act that Katta had done.

It was Lamson's spirit filled with hope and faith. Helen started believe in her own potential and this is what that brings the success in one's life.

Q 4. Describe the role of Helen's mother after Helen's illness.

हेलेन की बीमारी के बाद उसकी माँ का क्या योगदान था? वर्णन करें।

➤ हेलेन की माँ का हेलेन की जिंदगी का एक महत्त्वपूर्ण हिस्सा होना – हेलेन की बीमारी के बाद हेलेन का सबसे ज्यादा ख्याल रखना – हेलेन की शिक्षा और उसकी परवरिश का ख्याल रखना – जिंदगी का सच्चा साथी होना।

Ans. As we know, a mother is always concerned for the well– being of her children, Helen's mother was no exception. When Helen fell ill and afterwards when she lost her sight and hearing ability, her mother played a very crucial role in her life.

She managed to provide her the best teacher in the form of Miss Sullivan. She was totally conscious of all her needs and worries. She provided her schooling and gave her the opportunity to let herself feel free in her life. Not only this, but she was the one who was the closest to Helen all the time.

There is no doubt that her mother had shown such a degree of character and temperament that is really praise-worthly.

It was Helen's mother's resolution to equip her with education and she understood a painstaking task for doing it. Her affection and sympathy was with Helen and she never left her daughter in the state of emotional vaccum.

Q 5. How did Helen practice to develop her natural speech?

हेलेन ने अपने प्राकृतिक स्वर को विकसित करने के लिए किस तरह से अभ्यास किया ?

हेलेन द्वारा बोलने व सीखने का बहुत प्रयत्न करना – अपनी माँ के होठों पर हाथ रखकर बोलना सीखना – शब्दों के उच्चारण का अनुमान लगाना – स्वयं के गले व होठों पर हाथ रखना – कंपन की दिशा व गति का अनुमान लगाना – मिस फुलर के साथ भी यही प्रक्रिया बार-बार दोहराना।

Ans. It was not an easy decision for Helen to opt for learning the art of speaking. She would have to do intense practice for acquiring this skill. But, as she was determined to do so, she went for it. She had started it very early, when she had lost her ability to hear and see. She would sit in the lap of her mother and would try to spot the movement of her mother's lips.

She would even put her hand on her throat and lips to do the same. She would keep her hand when the piano was being played. Apart from this, she would keep her hands on the lips of Miss Fuller.

All of this was to develop her natural speech. She had set a benchmark for herself to overcome all the barriers in her life. Anything that could give her a feeling of sound was an unending joy and not a single moment was there when she resisted her from this. It was a continuous and evergoing process for her.

14

Helen Writes a Story, 'The Frost King'

Once Helen learns to speak, then she writes a story of her own, 'The Frost King' and this work makes her happy. After relating the story to her teacher, she reads it out to the members of her family.

Mr Anagnos Published Helen's Story

Helen sends a copy of the story 'The Frost King' to Mr Anagnos, who then publishes it in one of the Perkins Institution reports. This is one of the happiest moments for Helen. But her happiness is short lived as Helen is accused of plagiarism. It was discovered that a similar story 'The Frost Fairies" by Miss Margaret Canby had appeared before her 'The Frost King' in a book. After Helen's story was published, it was believed that Helen may have heard Miss Canby's story and had thus reproduced it as her own. This accusation deeply hurt Helen as she did not remember ever hearing 'The Frost Fairies'.

Mr Anagnos Feels Very Sad

Helen participated in the birthday celebration of George Washington. A teacher questions her about 'The Frost King' and Helen tells her that Miss Sullivan had talked to her about the works of 'Jack Frost'. This allows the teacher to believe that Helen had confessed her guilt and conveys this to Mr Anagnos.

Now, Mr Anagnos does not care for Helen's pleadings of love and innocence and he too accuses her of plagiarism. In the court, Helen is thoroughly questioned and the judges almost force her to acknowledge that she had indeed heard the story, 'The Frost Fairies'. At the end of the judgement, nothing is proved against Helen, but she is thoroughly hurt and humiliated.

हेलेन का कहानी लिखना 'द फ्रॉस्ट किंग'

जब Helen (हेलेन) बोलना सीख जाती है, तब वह The Frost King ('द फ्रॉस्ट किंग') नाम की अपनी कहानी लिखती है और यह कार्य उसे खुशी देता है। इस कहानी को अपनी शिक्षिका के सम्मुख संबोधित करने के पश्चात् हेलेन ने इसे अपने पूरे परिवार के सामने सुनाया।

हेलेन की कहानी का मि एनाग्नॉस के द्वारा छपवाना

हेलेन ने अपनी कहानी 'द फ्रॉस्ट किंग' को Mr Anagnos (मि एनाग्नॉस) के पास भेजा, जिन्होंने इस कहानी को Perkins Institute (परकिंस इंस्टीट्यूट) की एक रिपोर्ट में छपवा दिया। हेलेन के लिए यह सबसे खुशनुमा पलों में से एक था, लेकिन उसके लिए यह खुशी ज्यादा समय तक नहीं रही हेलेन पर Plagiarism (साहित्यिक चोरी) का आरोप लगाया गया। यह जानकारी प्राप्त की गई कि Miss Margaret Canby (मिस मार्ग्रेट केनबी) द्वारा लिखी गई समान कहानी The Frost Fairies ('द फ्रॉस्ट फेअरीज') उसकी कहानी के पहले ही प्रकाशित हो चुकी थी। हेलेन की कहानी के छपने के बाद यह माना गया कि हेलेन ने मिस केनबी की कहानी के बारे में सुना होगा और फिर इसे अपनी कहानी के तौर पर छपवा दिया होगा। इस आरोप ने हेलेन को बहुत दु:ख पहुँचाया, क्योंकि इससे पहले उसने कभी 'द फ्रॉस्ट फेअरीज' के बारे में नहीं सुना था।

मि एनाग्नॉस को अत्यधिक दु:ख होना

हेलेन George Washington (जॉर्ज वाशिंगटन) के जन्मदिन की पार्टी में शामिल हुई। वहाँ पर एक टीचर ने The Frost King ('द फ्रॉस्ट किंग') के बारे में पूछा, तो हेलेन ने बताया कि मिस सुलिवान ने Jack Frost ('जैक फ्रॉस्ट') के बारे में बताया था। उस टीचर ने इसे एक स्वीकृति मान ली और जाकर मि एनाग्नॉस को बताया कि हेलेन ने 'नकल' की स्वीकृति दी है।

अब मि एनाग्नॉस हेलेन की प्यार और मासूमियत की बातों की परवाह और उसके भोलेपन पर भरोसा नहीं करते और अब वे भी हेलेन की कहानी को साहित्यिक चोरी समझने लगे थे। अदालत में हेलेन से बहुत सारे सवाल-जवाब किए गए और उस पर जजों ने परोक्ष रूप से यह दबाव डाला कि उसने 'द फ्रॉस्ट फेअरीज' की कहानी सुनी है। मुकदमे के अंत तक कुछ भी साबित नहीं हुआ, परंतु हेलेन को अपमान और मानसिक कष्ट सहना पड़ा।

Word Meaning

Anxiety	– चिंता	Charm	– अच्छाई
Dreadful	– खतरनाक	Descriptions	– वर्णन
Retained	– याद रखना	Unconsciously	– बिना जाने-बूझे
Offspring	– उपज	Regretfully	– अफसोस के साथ
Impression	– सोच बनाना	Vividly	– अलग-अलग तरीके से
Annoyance	– नाराजगी	Astonished	– आश्चर्यचकित
Grieved	– तकलीफ देना	Disgraced	– शर्मिंदगी
weary	– थका हुआ	Masque	– संगीतमय नाटक
Oppressive	– जोरदार अपील	Confession	– स्वीकार करना
Deceived	– धोखा देना	Pleadings	– प्रार्थना
Admiration	– प्रशंसा	Acknowledge	– मानना
Reproachfully	– अस्वीकृति दिखाना	Scarcely	– शायद ही
Caresses	– प्यार भरा स्पर्श	Disposed	– हटा देना
Saturated	– परिपूर्ण	Devoid	– वंचित
Animated	– जीवंत	Marshal	– इकट्ठा करना
Legion	– बहुत ज्यादा	Texture	– सतह की प्रकृति
Crude	– अपरिष्कृत	Notions	– संकेत
Trammel	– रोकना	Frolics	– खुशी मनाना

Important Questions

Questions based on the Plot of the Chapter

Q 1. How did the publishing of the Helen's story, 'The Frost King' change her life ?

'द फ्रॉस्ट किंग' के छपने के बाद हेलेन की जिंदगी कैसे परिवर्तित हो गई?

हेलेन का बोलना सीख लेना – हेलेन द्वारा एक कहानी लिखना – हेलेन का मि एनाग्नॉस को अपनी कहानी भेजना – मि एनाग्नॉस द्वारा कहानी को परकिंस इंस्टीट्यूट की रिपोर्ट में छपवा देना – कहानी छपने पर दोनों का खुश होना – हेलेन पर नकल (साहित्यिक चोरी) का आरोप लगना – दोनों को भारी निराशा होना – हेलेन का इस खबर से बहुत दुःखी होना।

Ans. When Helen learnt to speak then she was very keen to express her desire in the forms of words. She started writing stories and it was keeping Mr Anagnos in her mind and to get the appreciation of her most dear friend. When she was done with the story then she read it aloud in front of the family. Family felt privileged. She dispatched her story to Mr Anagnos and he published it in the report of Perkins Institute.

It was a moment of pride for both, Mr Anagnos and to Helen. But, this pride soon meet its end as Helen was accused of the plagiarism. This hurt both of them and Helen was just disconsolable.

Helen started to see the life with different approach thinking that how cruel time goes at times! She was grieved above all these issues that were running all the while. It made her suffocate mentally and she didn't even think critically then.

Q 2. After Helen is accused of plagiarism, she presents certain instances when she could have heard the story, 'The Frost Fairies'. Elucidate.

नकल करने के आरोप के बाद हेलेन ने अपने बचाव में कुछ तथ्य रखे। उनका वर्णन कीजिए।

हेलेन की कहानी का प्रकाशित होना – हेलेन पर नकल करने का आरोप लगना – जाँच समिति द्वारा हेलेन से सवाल-जवाब करना – हेलेन का कहना कि उसने जैक फ्रॉस्ट की कहानियाँ पढ़ी हैं – हेलेन का नकल के आरोप से इंकार करना – हेलेन का दुःखी होना।

Ans. When Helen wrote the story 'The Frost King' then she was accused of the fact that she had plagiarised the story from the Canby's story as both have many things in common. Helen had to face a Panel of Judges for the same accusation.

The panel cross-questioned her about the event and she put herself with many instances to defend herself. She told that she had heard about the work of Jack Frost from her teacher Miss Sullivan, but she had never copied a single word from the story of Canby.

She had heard a bit of these stories too from Miss Sullivan, but she had never tried to reproduce the facts in anyway. Helen pleaded with genuine pouring out to the panel about her condition that she had not done that sin what they perceive to be plagiarism.

She told them clearly that hearing the story was another thing and it had nothing to do with that of producing in her own story and writing. But, none of the pleadings were accepted.

Helen Writes a Brief Account of Her Life

After 'The Frost King' incident, Helen spends the summer and winter with her family at Albama. She is now extra careful about what she writes and often wonders whether her writings would appear to be a copy of some other piece. Miss Sullivan restores Helen's confidence and persuades her to write for the Youth's Companion a brief account of her life. When she is just twelve years old.

Trip to Washington and Niagara Falls

Another main event of 1893 was Helen's trip to Washington. She also visits the Niagara Falls and the World Fair. The Niagara Falls impress Helen and she finds it difficult to express her emotions.

Visit to World Fair with Dr Graham Bell

In the summer of 1893, Helen visits the World Fair with Dr Bell and was delighted to touch the exhibits there. She liked to visit the Midway Plaisance which seemed like the Arabian Nights. Here she experienced India, Cairo and Viking ship-stories she had read in her books.

Mr Higinbotham-President of the World Fair

Mr Higinbotham, president of the World Fair, kindly gave her permission to touch the exhibits. At the Cape of Good Hope exhibit, she learnt about the process of mining diamonds. Dr Bell went everywhere with Helen and described the objects of greatest interest like the telephones, autophones, photographs and other inventions. They visited the anthropological department. Helen shrank from touching the Egyptian mummies.

हेलेन ने अपनी जीवनी संक्षेप में लिखी

The Frost King ('द फ्रॉस्ट किंग') वाली घटना के बाद Helen (हेलेन) ने अपनी सर्दी व गर्मी की छुट्टियाँ अपने परिवार के साथ Albama (अलबामा) में बिताई। वह अब अपनी लिखी हुई हर चीज पर ज्यादा ध्यान देती थी कि कहीं वह फिर से नकल के आरोप में न घिर जाए। Miss Sullivan (मिस सुलिवान) ने हेलेन का भरोसा वापस दिलाया और Youth's Companion (यूथ कंपैनियन) के लिए अपने जीवन की छोटी-सी कहानी लिखने के लिए समझाया, जब वह केवल बारह वर्ष की थी।

वाशिंगटन और नियाग्रा जलप्रपात का भ्रमण

1893 की एक अन्य मुख्य घटना हेलेन की Washington (वाशिंगटन) की यात्रा थी। उसने (Niagara Falls) नियाग्रा जलप्रपात और विश्व मेले का भी भ्रमण किया। हेलेन नियाग्रा जलप्रपात से बहुत ज्यादा प्रभावित हुई थी और वह अपनी भावनाओं को व्यक्त करने में कठिनाई महसूस कर रही थी।

डॉ ग्राह्य बेल के साथ विश्व मेले का भ्रमण

1893 की गर्मियों में हेलेन Dr Bell (डॉ बेल) के साथ World Fair (विश्व मेला) देखने गई और वहाँ पर रखी सारी Exhibitions (प्रदर्शनियों) को छूकर देखने पर हेलेन खुश हुई थी। उसे Midway Plaisance (मिडवे प्लेसन्स) में जाना पसंद था, जो Arabian Nights (अरेबियन नाइट्स) जैसा प्रतीत होता था। यहाँ पर वह India, Caira and Viking Ships (इंडिया, कैरो तथा वाइकिंग जहाज) जैसी कहानियों को अनुभव करती थी, जो कि उसने किताबों में पढ़ी थीं।

मि हिगिनबॉथम-वर्ल्ड फेयर के प्रेसीडेंट

वर्ल्ड फेयर के प्रेसीडेंट Mr Higinbotham (मि हिगिनबॉथम) ने हेलेन को प्रदर्शनी में रखे समान को छूने की इजाजत दी। Cape of Good Hope (केप ऑफ गुड होप) प्रदर्शनी में उसने हीरों के खनन के बारे में जानकारी प्राप्त की। डॉ बेल हेलेन के साथ हर जगह गए और उसे प्रत्येक चीज का; जैसे– टेलीफोन, ऑटोफोन, फोटोग्राफ और अन्य आविष्कार का वर्णन किया। वे दोनों मानव-विज्ञानी विभाग गए। हेलेन Egyptian Mummies (मिस की ममियों) को छूकर थोड़ी सिकुड़ (पीछे हटना) गई।

Word Meaning

Delight	– खुशी	Budded	– नई कोंपलें आना
Strewn	– सतह के ऊपर बिखरना	Crimson	– भगवा रंग (सुर्ख लाल)
Arbour	– वृक्षों की छाया	Scrupulous	– खासतौर पर
Tormented	– मानसिक कष्ट	Sensitiveness	– संवेदनशील
Prevented	– रोकना	Impish	– शरारती
Uneasiness	– बेचैनी	Disquietude	– चिंता
Consoled	– सांत्वना देना	Significance	– महत्त्व
Persuaded	– करना	Timidly	– डरपोक की तरह
Resolutely	– निश्चित रूप से	Gradually	– धीरे-धीरे
Emerged	– बाहर आना	Penumbra	– छाया

Important Questions

Questions based on the Plot of the Chapter

Q 1. Why was Helen still excessively scrupulous about everything she wrote?

हेलेन अपनी रचनाओं को लेकर ज्यादा सजग क्यों रहती थी? तब किसने उसे प्रेरित किया था?

↗ हेलेन पर एक बार नकल का आरोप लगना – कुछ भी लिखने से पहले भयभीत हो जाना – डर कि फिर से नकल का आरोप न लग जाए – हेलेन का लेखन कार्य बन्द कर देना – मिस सुलिवान के कहने पर दुबारा से लेखन कार्य शुरू करना।

Ans. Helen had been accused of plagiarism in an earlier case, but after that particular incident, she resisted herself from writing anymore. She had a thought that if she would write then it might again turn out to be someone else's writing. This fear was haunting enough to refrain her from writing. That's why, Helen was restraining herself from writing. When Miss Sullivan come to know about Helen's fear, she encouraged her to write without fear.

The consolation from Miss Sullivan helped her to achieve what she wanted for long. The fear that comes into the mind takes times to make its way. It becomes such a situation where one does not have mental peace.

Q 2. How does Helen make a trip around the world during her visit to the World's Fair with Dr Bell?

वर्ल्ड फेयर के दौरान हेलेन ने दुनिया का चक्कर कैसे लगाया था?

↳ हेलेन का वर्ल्ड फेयर जाना – मेले को करीब से देखने और महसूस करने का अवसर मिलना – अलग-अलग देशों से प्रदर्शनी का वहाँ आना – मेला घूमने के बाद हेलेन को लगना कि पूरी दुनिया देख ली गई हो – इस कारण हेलेन का मानना कि उसने पूरी दुनिया का चक्कर लगा लिया।

Ans. Helen went to the World Fair with Dr Bell. This fair was a place where she exhibits from all over the world were gathered and there was a lot of interest and enthusiasm in the minds of the people regarding the event and it couldn't be compared to any other. Helen made a trip all over the world virtually when she found exhibits from different countries and she loved it too. That's what she would be able to see had she been to every country, but this fair had given her all these opportunities without having to visit so many countries. That was the reason, that it was said that Helen had a trip around the world during her visit to the World Fair.

Helen was very much justified in saying that the scenic beauty that one can see when one goes out to see the world was seen by her in the World Fair was visible to Helen in the World Fair. She felt that the peculiar and prominent were available to her in a well defined premise giving her the feeling that she had seen everything offered by the world.

Q 3. Write a short note on Helen's experience aboard a Viking ship?

समुद्री जहाज (वाइकिंग) से जुड़े हेलेन के अनुभव का वर्णन करें।

↳ हेलेन का वाइकिंग शिप देखना – हेलेन के लिए एक सुखद व रोमांचक अनुभव होना – हेलेन को बेहद पसंद आना – हेलेन को अनुभव होना कि जहाज से किस तरह से चोरी होती होगी – हेलेन को बेहतरीन अनुभव मिलना – हेलेन की खुशी की सीमा न होना।

Ans. Viking ship used to be a pirate ship and she come to know how difficult it would be to use the ship for the purpose of making a theft. She felt the ultimate happiness in doing all this and she was overwhelmed by the feeling of this visit to the Viking ship. Her fascination for the visit was truly adorable. It is true that Viking was only a ship, but Helen learnt a good lesson from it that what people think awkward in the outside world even that needs meticulous planning for performing that. Viking ship gave her the same thought and that's why she was dead keen to see that ship. She had the feeling that the ship theft was not a child's game, but it needs effort. It was overall a pleasing and wonderful experience for her.

Q 4. Where was the Cape of Good Hope? What did Helen learn from this exhibit?

केप ऑफ गुड होप कहाँ है? हेलेन को इससे क्या सीखने का अवसर मिला?

↗ केप ऑफ गुड होप – दक्षिण अफ्रीका के पेरू में स्थित होना – खनिज लवणों के लिए मशहूर – हेलेन का उस जगह पर जाना – वहाँ जाकर उपयोग की जा रही मशीनरी को देखना – हेलेन को ज्ञात होना कि हर कीमती चीज को हासिल करने के लिए भारी कीमत अदा करनी।

Ans. Cape of Good Hope is located in the marine parts of South Africa. It is in Peru exactly adjacent to Capetown. The place is very rich in minerals like gold and diamonds. When Helen was there on visit, there she happened to see the process of mining and she even touched the machines. She got to know that it is not so easy to extract these costly items. She also got the idea that things that are precious require much effort to achieve them.

This was a subconscious and dominant thought of Helen. Helen must have thought that the name had been picked up with a lot of logic. It was really a good hope to get gold and diamond. Miners have always an anticipation of getting value for their effort and work by putting up their resources and money. Helen got the lesson that people sweat a lot when they are engaged in a work that gricks out valuable articles.

Questions based on the Character-Sketch

Q 5. Why did the president of the World Fair allow Helen to touch the exhibits? What does it reflect about his character?

वर्ल्ड फेयर के प्रेसीडेंट ने हेलेन को प्रदर्शनी छूने की इजाजत क्यों दी थी? इससे उसके कौन-से गुण का पता चलता है?

↗ विश्व मेले में हेलेन का जाना – प्रेसीडेंट द्वारा हेलेन को अनुमति मिलना कि वह चीजों को छूकर देख सके – प्रेसीडेंट द्वारा एक मिसाल कायम करना – उसके द्वारा सच्चे मानवीय गुणों का परिचय देना – किसी के चेहरे पर मुस्कान लाना – बहुत ही आनंददायक होना।

Ans. Helen was on her visit to the World Fair and she was excited about it. Whenever she happened to see anything, she wanted to feel it and it was necessary to have the permission of the president of the World Fair and he allowed her to do so. It shows that the president was a man of true spirit and he knew what it meant to bring cheer and happiness on the face of someone who is physically challenged.

He was a kind hearted man and he was the ambassador of humanitarian approach. His instincts were all divine. President was a man of golden heart and golden thought. He had a compatibility with the feelings of the people and he valued it just equal to life. When he gave permission to Helen to touch those exhibits he must not have thought even for a while because the it was true instinct of his heart. His conduct was praiseworthy and his deeds were solemn.

Q 6. Who was Dr Graham Bell? How did he prove to be an ideal companion? What knowledge did he impart to Helen?

डॉ. ग्राह्म बेल कौन थे? वह एक आदर्श साथी कैसे साबित हुए? उन्होंने हेलेन को क्या शिक्षा दी?

डॉ. बेल उच्चकोटि के व्यक्तित्व का प्रतिनिधित्व होना – उनका आविष्कारक, शिक्षक और बेहतरीन इंसान होना – हेलेन और डॉ. बेल विश्व मेले में गए – डॉ. बेल द्वारा उसे कई तरह की मशीनों की जानकारी देना – हेलेन की हर जिज्ञासा डॉ. बेल ने शान्त की – डॉ. बेल हेलेन के लिए एक वरदान साबित हुए।

Ans. Dr Graham Bell is a well-known personality in the world. He was a person of multi-dimensional traits being the inventor of the telephone, a teacher and a good human being. He was technically very sound and well versed is the machineries around him. Whenever, Helen found an interest in the surrounding machinery item, Dr Bell was always there to quench her curiosity. Helen enriched herself with many ideas and knowledge when she had a trip with Dr Bell. It was a great asset to Helen. Dr Bell revealed the old saying that one can't be thirsty when one is with river. Such was the case with Helen as she was moving with a living scientific legend. Helen was on the right track as she had the guidance of a distinguished and genuine personality.

Helen Learns Languages

By October 1893, Helen has read the histories of Greece, Rome and the United State of America. She already knows some French and reads with pleasure some of the good French writer's books. Now, Mr Irons, a neighbour and good Latin scholar teaches Helen Latin. Mr Irons reads to her Alfred Tennyson's "In Memoriam", which makes Helen understand an author's style. At first, Helen find Latin grammar absurd but later finds it a beautiful language.

हेलेन का भाषा सीखना

अक्टूबर, 1893 तक Helen (हेलेन) Greece, Rome and the United State of America (ग्रीस, रोम और संयुक्त राज्य अमेरिका) का इतिहास पढ़ चुकी थी। कुछ हद तक उसे French (फ्रेंच) का ज्ञान भी था और वह कुछ अच्छे फ्रेंच लेखकों की किताबें और उनकी रचनाएँ भी पढ़ लेती थी। हेलेन के पड़ोसी Mr Irons (मि आयरंस), जो एक अच्छे लैटिन के विद्वान् थे, उन्होंने हेलेन को लैटिन पढ़ाना शुरू किया। मि आयरंस ने उसे Alfred Tennyson (अल्फ्रेड टेनीसन) In Memoriam ('इन मेमोरियम') पढ़ाई, उसी दौरान हेलेन को एक लेखक के तरीकों का पता चला। प्रारंभ में हेलेन को Latin Grammar (लैटिन ग्रामर) अच्छी नहीं लगी, परंतु बाद में उसे लैटिन एक अच्छी भाषा लगने लगी।

Helen's Critical Analysis

When Helen developed an interest in the literature, she got to know the beauty that lies in the analysing of the text word by word. She would delight herself by literature all the time.

हेलेन द्वारा समीक्षात्मक आलोचना

जब हेलेन को साहित्य में रुचि आने लगी, वह पाठ के शब्दों के विश्लेषण की उस सुंदरता को जान गई। वह हर समय साहित्य के साथ आनंद प्राप्त कर सकती थी।

Word Meaning

Desultory	– असंगत	Technicalities	– तकनीकी
Slender	– दुबला-पतला	Considerable	– विचारनीय
Committed	– समर्पित	Critical	– विवेचनात्मक
Clasp	– गले लगाना	Unwilling	– इच्छा न होना
Absurd	– बेढंगा	Genitive	– अधिकारपूर्वक
Vertebrate	– कशेरुकी	Quadruped	– चौपाया
Mammalia	– स्तनधारी	Ceased	– रुक जाना
Evanescent	– धुंधला-सा दिखना	Fleeting	– तेजी से गुजरना
Flit	– रंगहीन	Capricious	– जिसकी भविष्यवाणी न की जा सके

Important Questions

Questions based on the Plot of the Chapter

Q 1. Helen finds Latin grammar absurd in the beginning but later develops an interest in it. Explain how this happens.

शुरुआत में लैटिन ग्रामर अरुचिकर लगने के बाद हेलेन ने बाद में इसमें रुचि कैसे विकसित कर ली?

➤ हेलेन की दिलचस्पी फ्रेंच भाषा में होना – हेलेन का फ्रेंच साहित्य भी पढ़ लेना – लैटिन ग्रामर की कक्षाएँ लेना – लैटिन में रुचि न होना – मि आयरंस की कोशिश कि हेलेन को लैटिन अच्छी लगने लगना।

Ans. Helen had an instinct with the French and she was able to read some of the best french writings, but when she was subjected to learning Latin grammar, it was obvious that she would find it absurd as her interest was in French and she was very new to Latin. But later on, Helen developed an interest in Latin too and it was all because of Mr Irons who induced that very current in him and after that Helen became very interested in Latin Mr Irons put up untiring devotion and effort in bringing the best out of her.

This event reflects that when a person does not find a piece interesting then if he gets the company of such a person, who can guide and elaborate the real stuff within that piece, it is inevitable that the former must develop an interest in that piece. This is what had happened in the case of Helen where Mr Irons did his best to bring out the same from her.

Q 2. What makes Helen understand the style of an author?

किस बात से हेलेन को लेखकों के तौर-तरीकों का पता चला?

हेलेन की दिलचस्पी शुरूआत से फ्रेंच भाषा में होना – फ्रेंच साहित्य पढ़ना – साहित्य पढ़ने के दौरान यह पता चलना कि लेखक का किस प्रकार सटीक तैयारी करना – शब्दों व संदर्भों की व्याख्या करना भी हेलेन ने सीखा।

Ans. Helen's interest in French leads her to the reading of some good books on French literature. When she read all of them, she started to appraise these kinds of writing and it all started with word-to-word analysis of the writings. By this way she was able to know the meanings and contexts of the words she also understood the style of author. This had been a greater achievement when she understood the Latin grammar too. She believed that authors have to plan their writings well in advance.

The best way to learn something is that one should start doing the thing or start seeing some maestro doing the same thing. Helen started to read the literature and in doing so she got to know the tone and the style of writing along with the needed orientation from the writer. She became aware of the fact that writers have to plan in their core about the material.

Q 3. Why did Helen delighted to learn various languages?

हेलेन अलग-अलग भाषाओं को क्यों सीखना चाहती थी?

हेलेन का शिक्षा में प्रारम्भ से रुचि लेना – बोलने की कला सीखने के बाद से ही फ्रेंच भाषा को पसंद करना – बाद में लैटिन सीखने के बाद उसमें भी दिलचस्पी लेना – हेलेन का कुछ फ्रेंच साहित्य भी पढ़ना – हेलेन की इच्छा बहुत सारी भाषाएँ सीखने की होना – ज्यादा से ज्यादा साहित्य पढ़ने की इच्छा होना।

Ans. Helen was deeply interested in education since her childhood and she never missed a chance of getting it. She had interest in French language since her knowing of the art of speaking and she had read a few books on the French language. When she was having her lesson in Latin grammar she had least of interest in it, but later on she developed a keen interest in it too. When she developed this interest, she found Latin to be interesting too. With this intention, she got the idea that each language has its own beauty and if she could learn many languages then she would be able to read much more. So, she wanted to learn many languages.

As people developed the fond and the taste about something then they wanted some more of that thing. Such was the case with Helen, who had developed the taste and fond for the languages and therefore she was striving for learning more and more languages so that the hunger can be compensated thoroughly.

Questions based on the Character-Sketch

Q 1. Who was Mr Irons? How did he prove to be helpful to Helen?

मि आयरंस कौन थे? वह हेलेन के लिए मददगार साबित कैसे हुए?

मि आयरंस का हेलेन के लैटिन भाषा के शिक्षक होना – मि आयरंस का एक ज्ञानपूर्ण व्यक्ति होना – उनका शिक्षण के प्रति उत्साह होना – शुरूआत में लैटिन में हेलेन को दिलचस्पी नहीं लेना – मि आयरंस द्वारा चीजों को बहुत आसान बना देना – हेलेन की हर मुश्किल आसान हो जाना – मि आयरंस का हेलेन के लिए बहुत ज्यादा मददगार साबित होना।

Ans. Mr Irons was Helen's teacher for Latin and he was giving lessons to Helen on Latin. Mr Irons was a knowledgeable person and he had great enthusiasm for teaching. When he was teaching Helen initially, Helen had least interest in learning Latin and Mr Irons reckoned it. He simplified the things for Helen and taught her very patiently. This made Helen learn the things easily that she was taking a bit difficult to learn. This was his immense character that made things pretty easy and simple for Helen. This is how Mr Irons proved to be very helpful to Helen.

Efforts of Mr Irons could well be compared with the fans on a football ground whose cheer invokes the palyer to make a goal. He invoked the same lust in Helen about learning the language. He did the task of simplification of the subject matter for Helen that she took with both the hands and understood the underlying facts in them. This was just the right approach from Mr Irons.

Helen's Visit to America

Helen attended the meeting at Chautauqua of the American Association to promote the teaching of speech to the deaf. Helen then goes to Wright-Humason School for the deaf in New York city in October, 1894. Helen also learns German and French, still dislikes arithmetic. Helen desires to speak like other people thus, works very hard.

हेलेन की अमेरिका यात्रा

Helen (हेलेन) ने बधिरों के भाषण की शिक्षा को बढ़ावा देने के लिए American Association (अमेरिकन एसोसिएशन) की Chautauqua पर एक बैठक में हिस्सा लिया। हेलेन अक्टूबर 1894 में बधिरों के लिए Wright-Humason School New York (राइट-ह्यूमैसन स्कूल न्यूयॉर्क) शहर चली गई। हेलेन ने German and French (जर्मन और फ्रेंच) भाषा भी सीखीं, परंतु वह अंकगणित को नापसंद करती थी। हेलेन की प्रबल इच्छा थी कि वह दूसरे लोगों की तरह ही बात करे, इसके लिए वह बहुत मेहनत कर रही थी।

Helen in Central Park

The two years in New York were happy ones for Helen. She enjoyed walking in the Central Park and loved to have it described every time she entered it. Before Helen leaves New York, the death of Mr John Spaulding, a philanthropist from Boston and Helen's benefactor passes away in February, 1896. His death saddens Helen and after her father's death, Mr Spaulding's death is the second one Helen has seen so far.

सेंट्रल पार्क में हेलेन

न्यूयॉर्क में बिताए दो साल हेलेन के लिए बहुत अच्छे समय में से एक थे। वह Central Park (सेंट्रल पार्क) में घूमना बहुत पसंद करती थी और वह जब भी वहाँ जाती तो उसके विषय में बताती। हेलेन के न्यूयॉर्क छोड़ने से पहले Boston (बोस्टन) के मनोविज्ञानी Mr John Spaulding (मि जॉन स्पाउलडिंग), जो हेलेन के लिए परोपकारी थे की मृत्यु फरवरी, 1896 में हो गई। इस मृत्यु से हेलेन को बहुत दुःख हुआ और अपने पिता की मृत्यु के बाद दूसरी बार हेलेन को सबसे ज्यादा दुःख मि स्पाउलडिंग की मृत्यु पर हुआ।

Word Meaning

Acquired	– हासिल करना	Indeed	– वास्तव में
Obliged	– कृतज्ञ	Ambition	– लक्ष्य
Accomplished	– पूरा करना	Inevitable	– अपरिहार्य
Pit falls	– कमियाँ	Frontier	– सीमा रेखा
Aggravated	– वृद्धि करना	Unflagging	– बाधा दूर करना
Picturesque	– बहुत ही अच्छी	Genuine	– वास्तविक
Congenial	– एक जैसे पसंद होना	Aspects	– पहलू
Excursion	– भ्रमण	Grandeur	– महानता
Palisades	– घेराबंदी	Tendencies	– इरादे
Cramping	– जगह कम पड़ना	Borne	– बर्दाश्त करना
Unobtrusive	– अपने आप का दिखावा न करना	Tender	– नाजुक व कोमल
		Vacancy	– सूनापन
Fraught	– व्याकुल		

Important Questions

Questions based on the Plot of the Chapter

Q 1. Which subjects and languages did Helen study? What was her experience during the course of study?

हेलेन कौन-सी भाषा और कौन-से विषय पढ़ती थी? पढ़ने के दौरान उसके अनुभव का वर्णन करें।

हेलेन का भाषा अध्ययन व विभिन्न विषयों का सीखना – जर्मन, लैटिन व फ्रेंच भाषा का अध्ययन करना – भौतिक भूगोल का भी अध्ययन करना – कुछ नयी भाषाओं का होना – नयी भाषाओं का हेलेन के लिए परेशानी होना – हेलेन की कड़ी मेहनत – मैडम ओलिवॉयर को हस्त वर्णमाला भाषा का ज्ञान न होना।

Ans. Helen used to learn many languages and a lot of subjects too. She was learning French, Latin, German as the languages and physical geography and literature as the subjects. Her teachers too made a very brave effort in accomplishing her goal and they were really patient and conscious about the development of Helen. With the sincere efforts of teachers, Helen learnt the things quite easily.

Helen had every kind of experience during her study of various languages and subjects. Some languages were very new to her and some were not. New ones created a trouble to her. Apart from it, one of her teachers Madam Olivier had not the level best knowledge of the manual alphabet, who was to teach her the art of lip reading.

Q 2. What pleasure did she get when she lived in New York?

न्यूयॉर्क प्रवास के दौरान हेलेन ने कैसे खुशी प्राप्त की थी?

↳ हेलेन का न्यूयॉर्क प्रवास करना – हेलेन का सुखद और मधुर यादों से भरा होना – हेलेन के लिए न्यूयॉर्क के सेंट्रल पार्क का स्मरणीय स्थल होना – सेंट्रल पार्क के बारे में लिखने की प्रबल इच्छा का होना – हडसन नदी के किनारे घूमना – हरियाली का आनंद लेना – मि जॉन के साथ की सुखद यादें।

Ans. Helen's visit to New York was filled with a lot of fun, joy and newities. It was just memorable for Helen. She would go to the Central Park in New York and would stay there for hours. She would try to write all the time whenever she entered the park. She was having immense affection for the place.

Her another favourite haunt was Hudson river where she used to sail and on several occasions, she would take a stroll to the greeneries on its bank. It all delighted, her very much. Another delight was the company of Mr John whom she admire the most.

One who has the appreciation for the part of nature even just for the slightest then he would enjoy being in the lap of the nature. Helen had that appreciation for nature since her childhood and when she entered the Central Park in New York, the desire sprut out from within core of the heart. That was one of the sources for an unending joy to Helen.

Question based on the Character-Sketch

Q 3. Who was Helen's French teacher? Did she know the manual alphabet? Why did Helen face great difficulty in reading her lips?

हेलेन की फ्रेंच शिक्षक कौन थी? क्या उन्हें प्रारम्भिक वर्णों का ज्ञान था? हेलेन को उनकी ओष्ठ भाषा को समझने में क्या कठिनाइयाँ आई थीं?

हेलेन की फ्रेंच शिक्षक मैडम ओलिवॉयर – मैडम की नियुक्ति हेलेन को फ्रेंच पढ़ाने और ओष्ठ भाषा का ज्ञान देने के लिए होना – मैडम के वर्ण का ज्ञान हेलेन के ज्ञान के स्तर का नहीं होना – हेलेन को सीखने में समस्या का सामना करना – सीखने का शुरूआती दौर होने के कारण और भी मुश्किलें आना।

Ans. Madam Olivier was Helen's French teacher. She was appointed to teach Helen French. She was also responsible for developing the ability of lip reading and speech.

But, it all was closer to none because Olivier was not aware of the manual alphabet that she had to teach. Moreover, Helen faced too much difficulty in reading her lips properly and she failed in all her made efforts.

Since, Helen was a beginner therefore, it becomes even more challenging for her to learn the prescribed things.

She was not very well adapted to the lips reading. As Helen was completely dependant upon her teacher for the development of the skill that she wished to.

The difficulty aroused due to the incompatibility of her teacher too, who was not very good at the manual alphabet which was the main tool for learning. The problem was specific in nature.

18

Helen Goes for Higher Education

In October, 1896, Helen enters the Cambridge School for Young Ladies. Helen had a keen interest to get into Harvard and thus worked very hard for achieving her goal. At Cambridge, Helen studied along with students who could hear and see, so had to put in extra effort at to the study material.

Miss Sullivan could not space out in her hand all the books. Since it was difficult to get the books embossed in Braille, Miss Sullivan would read and re-read notes for Helen.

Helen Makes New Friends

At Cambridge, Helen makes new friends, who can hear and see and some of them even try to learn her hand language. They all live like a well connected family. Helen's younger sister, Mildred too joins her at Cambridge and they are very happy to be together.

Helen Passes in Preliminary Examinations for Radcliffe

Helen takes the preliminary examinations for Radcliffe from 29th June to the 3rd of July in 1897. She choose German, French, Latin, English, Greek and Roman history as her subjects. She passes in all these subjects and even receives 'honours' in German and English.

Mr Gilman-A Great Helper

Helen was really obliged to Mr Gilman for his immense support that he had given her in the period of examinations. She confesses it, that without his support this would not be possible any way.

हेलेन का उच्च शिक्षा प्राप्त करने के लिए जाना

अक्टूबर, 1896 में Helen (हेलेन) ने Cambridge (कैम्ब्रिज) स्कूल में दाखिला लिया, जो युवा लड़कियों के लिए था। Harvard (हावर्ड) में प्रवेश पाने के लिए हेलेन गहरी रुचि रखती थी और वह इसके लिए कड़ी मेहनत कर रही थी। हेलेन ने कैम्ब्रिज में उन बच्चों के साथ अध्ययन किया, जो देख और सुन सकते थे अत: हेलेन को पढ़ाई में बहुत मेहनत करने की जरूरत थी।

Miss Sullivan (मिस सुलिवान) सारी किताबों को उसके हाथों पर नहीं समझा सकती थी। यहाँ तक कि सारी किताबों को Braille (ब्रेल लिपि) (उभरी हुई भाषा) में भी बदलना कठिन था, मिस सुलिवान हेलेन के लिए नोट्स को पढ़ती और पुन: पढ़ती थी।

हेलेन के नए दोस्त बनना

कैम्ब्रिज में हेलेन ने नए दोस्त बनाए, जो सब सुन और देख सकते थे तथा उनमें से कुछ ने तो उसकी हाथों वाली भाषा में बात करने की कोशिश की। वे सब एक परिवार के जैसे रहते थे। हेलेन की छोटी बहन Mildred (मिल्ड्रेड) भी कैम्ब्रिज में गई और वे एक साथ रहकर बहुत खुश थे।

रेडक्लिफ की प्रारंभिक परीक्षा में हेलेन का सफल हो जाना

हेलेन ने 29 जून से 3 जुलाई, 1897 तक Radcliffe (रेडक्लिफ) की प्रारंभिक परीक्षा दी। उसने German, French, Latin, English, Greek and Rome (जर्मन, फ्रैंच, लैटिन, इंग्लिश, ग्रीक और रोम) के इतिहास को अपने विषय के रूप में चुना। उसने सभी परीक्षाओं को पास कर लिया था तथा जर्मन और इंग्लिश में तो उसे Honours ('सम्मान') भी प्राप्त हुआ था।

मि गिलमैन-एक महान् मददगार

परीक्षा के दौरान Mr Gilman (मि गिलमैन) द्वारा दी गई अपार सहायता के लिए हेलेन उनकी आभारी थी। वह यह भी मानती थी कि बिना उनकी मदद के यह किसी भी तरह से संभव नहीं था।

Word Meaning

Earnest	– गंभीर		Impelled	– राजी कर लेना
Opposition	– विरोधी, विपक्षी		Declaration	– घोषणा करना
Interpret	– वर्णन करना		Drilled	– गहराई तक
Evident	– स्पष्ट होना		Critical	– संकटपूर्ण
Drawbacks	– कमी		Tedium	– थकान होना
Conceive	– समझना		Inadequate	– अपर्याप्त
Laboriously	– मेहनत से		Drudgery	– गुलामी

Important Questions

Questions based on the Plot of the Chapter

Q 1. In spite of certain advantages at the Cambridge School, there were serious drawbacks to Helen's progress. Elaborate.

कैम्ब्रिज स्कूल में कुछ सहूलियतें थीं, तो कुछ मुश्किलें भी थीं। वर्णन करिए।

↙ हेलेन के लिए कैम्ब्रिज स्कूल लाभकारी होना – कैम्ब्रिज सामान्य बच्चों का स्कूल होना – हेलेन के लिए थोड़ी मुश्किलें होना – सारी किताबें ब्रेल लिपि में परिवर्तित करनी मुश्किल होना – हेलेन का मिस सुलिवान पर निर्भर रहना – हेलेन की तरक्की में बाधा होना – शिक्षा का माहौल अच्छा होना।

Ans. There is no doubt about the fact that the Cambridge school was a lot beneficial to Helen. But despite these advantages there were some drawbacks too. Cambridge was a school for normal students, but Helen was physically challenged. That's why she had to work very hard to be equal to those of the normal students. Most of all, all the books couldn't be embossed in the braille script which was another drawback.

Helen had to depend on Miss Sullivan for her help in understanding what was taught in the class. So, Helen was not very much in the position of advantage. Helen had to face the fierce competition from the normal children, who used to out perform Helen as she was physically challenged. There was a good educational environment that had helped Helen in developing the true spirit so that she could be able to learn what she intended to. Helen's zest for learning could meet the right end then.

Q 2. Explain the method of the preliminary examinations for Radcliffe which Helen appeared for.

रेडक्लिफ की प्रारंभिक परीक्षा, जिसमें हेलेन शामिल हुई थी, के तरीके का वर्णन करें।

रेडक्लिफ में प्रारंभिक परीक्षा होना – मि गिलमैन की मदद से हेलेन का परीक्षा में शामिल होना – मि गिलमैन द्वारा शब्दों व प्रश्नों का हाथ में उच्चारण करना – हेलेन का उत्तर लिखना – उत्तर लिखने के बाद महत्त्वपूर्ण सुधार करना – हेलेन का परीक्षा उत्तीर्ण करना।

Ans. Helen appeared an examination for Radcliffe. In fact, her purpose of enrollment in the Cambridge school was a way to Radcliffe. As she was physically challenged the accoutrements for the exams were to be different than that of the normal students. She was provided with the support of Mr Gilman.

She was given a separate room to appear for exam. Words were being spelt into her hands and she used to write her answer. when her answers were over she was made to listen it and the needed change was made into it. This was the way of appearing in preliminary examination.

Yet, Helen was not very comfortable with the pattern as she had to abolish the customary trend of examination. Most of all, she had no helping hand in terms of Miss Sullivan who was a great asset for her.

The examiner did not allow Miss Sullivan to assist Helen in that exam. The new way was creating a mental zone of discomfort for Helen.

19

Difficult Period for Helen

Although Helen was full of hope and determination at her second year at the Gilman school, she had to face many difficulties. Many of the books she needed to study had not been embossed in time.

She needed a Braille writer and had a problem with algebra and geometry as they required geometrical figures, which Helen could not see.

Mr Gilman Feels Helen is Overworked

Mr Gilman has begun to remonstrate with Miss Sullivan that Helen was overworked and he felt that she should complete her college in seven years instead of five.

Helen did not like the plan and she wanted to complete college along with her classmates. Finally, Helen's mother withdrew Helen and her sister Mildred from Cambridge school.

Mr Keith-Helen's New Tutor

Mr Keith of Cambridge is Helen's new tutor and under his guidance her preparation for college continues without interruption.

Helen finds his personal tution much more pleasant and easier than receiving instructions in class. In 1899, Helen took the final examination for Radcliffe College.

हेलेन के लिए एक मुश्किल समय

Gilman School (गिलमैन स्कूल) के दूसरे साल में Helen (हेलेन) बहुत खुश और आशा से भरी हुई थी, परंतु उसे बहुत सारी मुश्किलों का भी सामना करना पड़ा था। उसकी पढ़ाई में काम आने वाली बहुत-सी किताबें समय पर उपलब्ध नहीं हो पाई थीं।

उसे एक Braille (ब्रेल) लेखक चाहिए था, क्योंकि ज्यामितीय और रेखागणित में उसे कुछ कठिनाइयाँ थीं, क्योंकि ये विषय ज्यामितीय संरचनाओं पर आधारित होते हैं, जिन्हें हेलेन नहीं देख सकती थी।

मि गिलमैन को लगना कि हेलेन ज्यादा परिश्रम कर रही है

Mr Gilman (मि गिलमैन) को ऐसा लगा कि हेलेन अपने लक्ष्य को पूरा करने के लिए ज्यादा परिश्रम कर रही है और उसने Miss Sullivan (मिस सुलिवान) से कहा कि उसे कॉलेज के लिए पाँच वर्ष के स्थान पर सात वर्ष मिलने चाहिए।

लेकिन हेलेन को यह सुझाव पसंद नहीं आया और उसकी इच्छा थी कि वह अपने दूसरे दोस्तों की तरह ही समय पर कॉलेज पूरा करे। अंतत: हेलेन की माँ ने हेलेन और उसकी बहन Mildred (मिल्ड्रेड) को Cambridge (कैम्ब्रिज) स्कूल से निकाल लिया।

मि कीथ-हेलेन के नए ट्यूटर

कैम्ब्रिज स्कूल के Mr Keith (मि कीथ) हेलेन के नए ट्यूटर थे और उनके संरक्षण में ही हेलेन ने अपनी कॉलेज की तैयारी बिना किसी रुकावट के शुरू कर दी थी।

हेलेन को उनका क्लास से ज्यादा निजी तौर पर पढ़ाना आसान और अच्छा लगा। हेलेन ने 1899 में Radcliffe (रेडक्लिफ) की आखिरी परीक्षा दी।

Word Meaning

Confronted	– सामना करना	Unforeseen	– पहले न देखा हुआ
Apparatus	– सामान	Interpret	– वर्णन करना
Hypothesis	– परिकल्पना	Obstacles	– बाधाएँ
Betrayed	– धोखा दिया	Crooked	– टेढ़ा-मेढ़ा
Renewed	– दुबारा से नया करना	Defy	– खुले तौर पर विरोध करना
Comprehend	– समझना	Aptitude	– क्षमता
Vexing	– चिंतित करना	Remonstrae	– विरोध करना
Earnest	– गंभीर	Protestations	– विरोधाभास
Recitations	– पाठ करना	Perplexing	– उधेड़बुन की स्थिति
Indisposition	– अस्वस्थता	Renderd	– कारक
Whittling	– कम करना	Forbearing	– धैर्यवान
Exhausted	– थका हुआ	Proctor	– विश्वविद्यालय की अनुशासनाधिकारी
Sorely	– बिल्कुल तौर पर		
Dismay	– निराशा	Notation	– संकेत
Complicated	– उलझा हुआ	Distressed	– नाखुश
Forebodings	– मुश्किल की उम्मीद करना	Morrow	– अगले दिन
Accustomed	– आदत	Propositions	– कथन
Relied	– भरोसा करना	Consequently	– परिणामस्वरूप
Wits	– बुद्धिमानी	Peculiar	– विचित्र
Surmount	– जीत लेना	Consolation	– सांत्वना देना

Important Questions

Questions based on the Plot of the Chapter

Q 1. Why did Helen's mother withdraw Helen and Mildred from Cambridge school?

हेलेन की माँ ने हेलेन और मिल्ड्रेड को कैम्ब्रिज स्कूल से क्यों निकाल लिया?

➔ मि गिलमैन को अहसास होना कि हेलेन का अतिरिक्त मेहनत करना – हेलेन की इच्छा कॉलेज को तय समय पर पूरा करना – मि गिलमैन और मिस सुलिवान के बीच इस बात को लेकर विवाद होना – मि गिलमैन का मानना कि हेलेन कॉलेज को सात साल में पूरा करे – विरोधाभास की वजह से हेलेन की माँ द्वारा स्कूल से वापस बुला लेना।

Ans. Helen and Mildred both were studying at the Cambridge school. Miss Sullivan was also with Helen to assist her in studies. Mr Gilman, there, thought that Helen had been overworked and she should complete her college in seven years instead of five years. When Helen got to know about this plan, she was on the opposite side. It resulted into the constant remonstration between Mr Gilman and Miss Sullivan. It lead to nothing, but the conflict when came to the knowledge of Helen's mother, she came up with another idea and she decided to withdraw Helen and Mildred from the school.

In a sense this withdrawl was a right and fair step from Helen's mother. Helen's mother knew that there was fierce difficulties in the Cambridge school and Helen would not be able to cope up with that very well and if she was to withdraw from there and proper attention is given on the studies of Helen then the desired result may be achieved soon.

Q 2. How did Helen overcome the obstacles placed before her when she took the final examinations for Radcliffe College?

रेडक्लिफ कॉलेज की आखिरी परीक्षा में हेलेन के सामने क्या मुश्किलें आई थीं?

रेडक्लिफ की आखिरी परीक्षा में हेलेन का शामिल होना – हेलेन के सामने कई दिक्कतें आना – हेलेन को संकेत अमेरिकन में दिया जाना – मिस सुलिवान का हेलेन के साथ न होना – मिस सुलिवान की जगह कोई नया इंसान होना – हेलेन को गणित में समस्या होना – हेलेन द्वारा एक ही उदाहरण को बार-बार पढ़ना – प्रक्रिया में बहुत समय लगना और बहुत मुश्किलें आना।

Ans. Helen worked very hard to complete her college on time. For this, she appeared in the final exam of Radcliffe College. She had studied languages and mathematics in the braille script. When she appeared in the exam, she was made apart from Miss Sullivan. Moreover, a stranger was placed before her. She had been provided with American notations for braille and that was another obstcle to her. She was not at home with those notations but she got none as an explanation, that made her progress a bit slow and she had to read the examples more and more to solve the questions. That's how there were obstacles. When a person is not very familiar with the condition, arising of the difficulties is obvious. As Helen was new to the American notations so she had to face the obvious challenge while appearing the exam for Radcliffe. Another asset Miss Sullivan was also not with Helen adding up to the problems of Helen considerably.

Q 3. How did Helen start her second year at Gilman school?

गिलमैन स्कूल में दूसरे साल की पढ़ाई हेलेन ने कैसे शुरू की ?

↗ हेलेन का गिलमैन कॉलेज में दूसरा साल होना – आशा व उम्मीद के साथ शुरू करना – आशा का थोड़ा धुंधला होना – हेलेन को ब्रेल लिपि समझने में दिक्कत आना – संकेतों का गणित में काम न आना – दूसरे साल में हेलेन का मूल तौर पर गणित पढ़ना – गणित हेलेन के लिए अरुचिकर विषय होना।

Ans. Helen started her second year at Gilman School with a lot of hope and determination. She was enthusiastic about her progress and study. But this zeal came to a sudden halt when there was a difficulty for her in learning due to the lack of the braille script and the books were also not upto her expectation that she could read it well. Mr Gilman added to her perplexities by saying that she had to study mathematics in the second year and Helen disliked that subject. All these were happening in the life of Helen in the second year at Gilman's.

Helen started with a fair amount of hope and anticipation at the Gilman's in the second year. This lightening hope started fading with the continuous argument between Mr Gilman and Miss Sullivan. Mathematics added fuel to the fire and Helen's worries were at the seventh sky. It was such a mixture of hope and pessimism that Helen was just swaying in between these two like a boat sways in the midst of a river.

Q 4. Why did Helen feel that mathematics was most difficult for her to understand?

हेलेन गणित को सबसे मुश्किल विषय क्यों मानती थी ?

↗ हेलेन की गणित में बहुत कम रुचि – ब्रेल लिपि की मदद से भी इसे समझना मुश्किल – ब्रेल में चित्र सटीक नहीं आना – दूसरे साल में हेलेन का मुख्य विषय गणित होना – हेलेन की सबसे बड़ी समस्या – बिना किसी की मदद के इसे समझ पाना मुश्किल होगा।

Ans. Helen had very least interest in mathematics. She disliked this subject from the very beginning, but in the Gilman's in the second year, she had to study maths principally. She feared the idea because she had no availability of braille script with her and without it, she would not be able to do that efficiently. Above all these, she hated the geometrical figures and she could not understand it well. Braille was not enough to curtail all her problems in mathematics even. Summing up all these, Helen thought that maths is the most difficult one to understand.

Obviously, maths had got a reputation that it could trouble anyone even a normal student and if the student is not normal then it may pose a bigger challenge even. This way maths becomes a tid bit to a learner. Another issue is that braille script had not much advancements for this subject therefore the trouble arises more and more.

Question based on the Character-sketch

Q 5. Who was Mr Keith? How did he teach Helen mathematics?

मि कीथ कौन थे? उन्होंने हेलेन को गणित कैसे पढ़ाया?

मि कीथ का कैम्ब्रिज स्कूल से आए हुए हेलेन के शिक्षक होना – मि कीथ द्वारा हेलेन को गणित पढ़ाना – उनका गणित को बड़ी आसानी से समझाना – प्रत्येक दिन हेलेन को काम देना और उसमें महत्त्वपूर्ण सुधार करना – प्रश्नों का स्तर आसान बनाकर हेलेन को समझाने की कोशिश करते – हेलेन के लिए काम आसान कर देना – गणित हेलेन को अब रुचिकर लगना।

Ans. Mr Keith was a teacher from Cambridge, who had come to teach Helen mathematics. He would come twice a week and would explain Helen what she failed to understand in the previous class. He would also assign new work, check the previous assignment and then return to his place with the braille typewriter to make necessary arrangements in the work done by Helen. Mr Keith paid extra attention during the classes of algebra and he would make the problems small enough so that Helen could well understand that. This way, maths was made too easy to understand for Helen.

Mr Keith is an example that maths is a subject of thinking and idea. He made it as a sum of thoughts and ideas leading to a better reading device. He proved that nothing could be so big if there are better ideas and innovations come by the gateway of thinking and it must be national and positive.

Helen Enters Radcliffe College

Hard work and focus pay off and Helen enters Radcliffe college but after a year of study under Mr Keith, Helen is excited and happy and she is keen to compete with those who can see and hear. Soon, Helen realises that there are many difficulties in her path to achieve what she aims for.

हेलेन का रेडक्लिफ कॉलेज में प्रवेश

Helen (हेलेन) की कड़ी मेहनत रंग लाई और Mr Keith (मि कीथ) के संरक्षण में एक साल का अध्ययन पूरा करने के बाद उसे Radcliffe (रेडक्लिफ) कॉलेज में प्रवेश मिल गया तथा हेलेन बहुत खुश और उत्सुक थी कि अब उसे सुनने और देखने वाले बच्चों के साथ प्रतियोगिता करने का अवसर मिलेगा। जल्द ही हेलेन को आभास हो गया कि जो वह पाने की इच्छा रखती है, उस रास्ते में उसके लिए बहुत सारी कठिनाइयाँ हैं।

Helen Faces Challenges at College

Since Helen was tutored privately by Miss Sullivan and later by Mr Keith, she soon discovered that it was a disadvantage to go to college. Among many students in the class, it was not possible for Helen to get the individual attention. She also felt that one goes to college to learn not to think.

कॉलेज में हेलेन का मुश्किलों से सामना

हेलेन को निजी तौर पर Miss Sullivan (मिस सुलिवान) ने और बाद में मि कीथ ने पढ़ाया था, जल्द ही उसे पता चल गया कि कॉलेज में यह उसके लिए नुकसान था। कक्षा में बहुत से विद्यार्थियों के होने की वजह से हेलेन पर व्यक्तिगत रूप से ध्यान देना मुश्किल था। उसे यह भी लगा कि कॉलेज में लोग सोचने नहीं, बल्कि सीखने आते हैं।

Word Meaning

Potent	– सक्षम	Persuasion	– राजी करना
Pleadings	– प्रार्थना	Impelled	– मजबूर करना
Obstacles	– बाधाएँ	Overcome	– जीत लेना
Banished	– बाहर निकालना	Debarred	– मनाही
Bypaths	– दूसरे रास्ते	Eagerness	– उत्सुकता
Tangible	– निश्चितता	Wisdom	– बुद्धिमत्ता
Lyceum	– पाठशाला	Faded	– बेरंग व बेजान
Commune	– बातचीत करना	Portals	– दरवाजा
Solitude	– अकेलापन	Whispering	– धीमी आवाज

Important Questions

Question based on the Plot of the Chapter

Q 1. Why did Helen remember her first day at Radcliffe college?

हेलेन रेडक्लिफ कॉलेज के अपने पहले दिन को क्यों याद करती है?

↳ हेलेन का कॉलेज में दाखिला लेना – हेलेन के द्वारा कठिन मेहनत करना – कॉलेज की आखिरी परीक्षा पास कर लेना – वर्षों की तमन्ना पूरी हो जाना – कॉलेज में प्रवेश मिलना – बहुत सारे खुशनुमा चेहरे देखना – हेलेन का बहुत ज्यादा खुश होना।

Ans. Helen had been striving for long to get herself enrolled in the college. She worked very hard for this and didn't leave any stone unturned. When she passed the final exam of the Radcliffe with her own effort then she was overwhelmed by the feeling. She thought that she would get the chance to study with the normal students and she loved that feeling.

She entered the college and felt its virbrant environment the very first day. She saw a lot of energetic and enthusiastic faces and then she was on the top of the world. No doubt, when a dream that has been cherished for long comes true, then there is no limit to one's happiness. One remembers the day when one struggled hard to accomplish the desired goal. Helen also felt satisfied when she looked back at the days of her struggle.

Books Mean a Lot to Helen

Helen depended on books not only for pleasure and wisdom but also for the knowledge. In May 1887, she had read the first story. As she read her vocabulary increased and she slowly learnt the meaning of many words. 'Little Lord Fauntleroy' was one of the first books she read and enjoyed it thoroughly.

Helen's Reading of Shakespeare's Play

'Macbeth' of Shakespeare impressed her most. For a long time the ghosts and witches haunted her in dreams. She read 'King Lear' after 'Macbeth'. The two others characters that Helen liked very much were of Shylock and Satan.

Helen Reads Other Authors too

Helen also reads novels and poems of the 19th century by French writers. She loved Mark Twain, famous author of 'The Adventures of Tom Sawyer' and 'Adventures of Huckleberry Finn.'

Word Meaning

Scarcely	– शायद ही		Fascinated	– आकर्षित
Retained	– बरकरार रखना		Clue	– मदद देना
Consequence	– परिणाम		Poring	– से होकर जाना
Existence	– अस्तित्व		Solemn	– पवित्र
Hastened	– जल्दीबाजी में		Swarmed	– झुंड में उड़ना
Fastened	– बँधा हुआ		Insisted	– दबाव देना
Balmy	– आरामदायक		Tang	– खुशबूदार
Keen	– उत्सुक		Intensity	– अधिकता
Tedious	– थका देने वाला		Vivid	– बहुरंगी
Mutable	– बदल सकने लायक		Kinship	– भाईचारा
Exclusion	– हटाना		Seldom	– शायद

हेलेन के लिए किताबों का महत्त्व

Helen (हेलेन) सिर्फ आनंद एवं बुद्धिमता के लिए ही नहीं किताबों पर निर्भर थी परंतु ज्ञान के लिए भी। 1887 में उसने पहली कहानी पढ़ी थी। लगातार किताबे पढ़ने से उसका शब्द ज्ञान बढ़ने लगा और कई नए शब्दों के अर्थ भी उसे समझ आने लगे थे। 'Little Lord Fauntleroy' ('लिटिल लॉर्ड फॉउन्टरॉय') उसकी पहली किताबों में से एक थी जिसे उसने पूरे अच्छी तरह से पढ़ा था।

हेलेन का शेक्सपियर की कहानियाँ पढ़ना

Shakespeare (शेक्सपियर) की Macbeth (मैकबेथ) ने उसे अत्यधिक प्रभावित किया। भूत एवं डायन ने लंबे समय तक सपनों में उसे डराया। मैकबेथ के बाद उसने King Lear (किंग लियर) का अध्ययन किया। Shylok (शॉयलक) एवं Satan (सॅटॉन) दो अन्य पात्र थे, जिन्हें हेलेन ने अत्यधिक पसंद किया।

हेलेन दूसरे लेखकों को भी पढ़ती

हेलेन 19वीं शताब्दी के फ्रैंच लेखकों के द्वारा लिखे गए कविता और उपन्यासों को स्वयं पढ़ती थी। The Adventure of Tom Sawyer ('एडवेंचर ऑफ टॉम स्वॉयर') और Adventures of Huckleberry Finn ('एडवेंचर ऑफ हकल बेरी फिन') के मशहूर लेखक Mark Twain (मार्क ट्वेन) को वह बहुत पसंद करती थी।

Fables	– दंत कथाएँ		Restrained	– वश में रखना
Satirical	– मजाकिया लहजा		Momentous	– महत्त्वपूर्ण
Genuine	– वास्तविक		Subtle	– कोमल
Conception	– विचार		Antiquity	– पुरातन
Shrine	– पवित्र स्थल		Tribe	– जनजाति
Demigods	– अर्द्धमानव		Wickedness	– दुष्ट बुद्धि
Paradise	– स्वर्ग		Responsive	– प्रतिक्रियात्मक
Odious	– दुष्कर		Impositions	– दबाव देना

Important Questions

Questions based on the Plot of the Chapter

Q 1. Why did Helen enjoy reading herself?

हेलेन को पढ़ना इतना पसंद क्यों था?

हेलेन का बचपन से ही एक उत्सुक पाठक होना – पढ़ने के लिए हमेशा प्रयासरत रहना – हेलेन का अपने को पढ़ाई में व्यस्त रखना – हेलेन के लिए पढ़ाई का ज्ञानवर्धक और मनोरंजक होना – पढ़ाई द्वारा हेलेन की जिंदगी के खालीपन को मिटा देना – पढ़ाई से हेलेन में नई स्फूर्ति आना।

Ans. Helen was a very keen learner and above that, a keen reader. She was fond of reading since her childhood and she made all possible efforts to achieve that.

She would involve herself to reading because it was not only her way to acquire more knowledge, but her favourite pastime too. It filled the isolation and vaccum of her life. She entertained herself by reading.

Reading kept her busy so that the awkward feelings would not enter her life. That's why, Helen enjoyed reading by herself. There was another reason why Helen loved reading by herself.

As she was physically challenged she had no friends at all. In the absence of friends, She needed something to preoccupy herself with. This way she also remained in a good mental state. It not only amused her, but also engrossed her.

Q 2. While reading books, Helen did not like certain things. Mention them.

पुस्तकों को पढ़ने के दौरान हेलेन को कुछ बातें अच्छी नहीं लगती थी। वर्णन करें।

➤ हेलेन की दिलचस्पी पढ़ाई में होना – हेलेन को कुछ बातों पर ऐतराज होना – हेलेन को किताबों में जानवरों का मानवीकरण पसंद न होना – हेलेन को जानवरों से लगाव होना पर मानवीकरण में दिलचस्पी नहीं – हेलेन शेक्सपियर की कहानियों के दो किरदारों को भी वह नापसंद करना – किरदार नकारात्मक प्रभाव के होना।

Ans. Helen had a very deep and keen interest in reading the books. She never missed a chance to read as it used to delight her altogether but, there were certain things or works that she hated to read. She did not like all the things that she read. She would avoid reading a piece of writing if it carried a caricature of men as animals. She loved animals, but when they are shown as caricatures, it was intolerable for her.

Apart from this, she did not like Shylock and Satan even if they tried to be good as their first impression was not good. Books when become a matter of taste and a matter of interest then people associate their likes and dislikes with them Helen was on the same ground, associated herself with the books and what she hated in her life she hated the same in the books too.

Helen Loves the Country and Outdoor Sports

One should not conclude that Helen's only pleasure was reading. She loved the countryside and thoroughly enjoyed outdoor sports. As a little girl, she had learnt to row and swim. Rowing and canoeing were her favourite water sports. She sailed in the summer of 1901 when she visited Nova Scotia in Canada. One summer she spent time in one of the most charming villages in New England.

City life-A Struggle

Unlike the country life where one gets to see the best of nature, the city life is a struggle and sadness Helen. The loud noises, the crowd and the narrow streets where poor people live, disturb Helen and she wonders why there is this huge gap between the poor and the rich. She does not understand why people are so materialistic and why the fortunate do not help their poor brothers.

Museums and Art Stores

Helen loved to spin on her bicycle and she had many dogs who accompanied her while she went for walks or cycling. In rainy days, she played indoor games. Helen was a friendly person and enjoyed the company of other children. She told them stories and taught them different games. She enjoyed going to art stores where she could feel the heart beats of ancient Greeks in the marble Gods and Goddesses.

Helen Feels Lonely at Times

At sometimes Helen feels a sense of isolation, which enfolds her like a cold mist. Hope comes with a smile and whispers, "There is joy in self forgetfulness"

हेलेन का गाँव और बाहर के खेलों को पसंद करना

यह निष्कर्ष नहीं निकाला जा सकता कि पढ़ना ही Helen (हेलेन) की एकमात्र रुचि थी। उसको गाँव बहुत पसंद थे और बाहर के खेलों में उसकी बहुत ज्यादा दिलचस्पी थी। बचपन में ही उसने तैरना और नाव चलाना सीख लिया था। पानी के खेल Rowing and Canoeing (नाव चलाना व कैनोइंग) उसे अत्यधिक पसंद थे। 1901 की गर्मियों के दौरान वह Canada (कनाडा) में Nova Scotia (नोवा स्कॉटिया) गई थी। एक बार उसने New England (न्यू इंग्लैंड) के एक सबसे सुंदर गाँव में अपनी गर्मियाँ बिताई थीं।

शहरी जीवन–एक अनवरत संघर्ष

हेलेन के लिए शहरी जीवन एक संघर्ष और दु:ख है, इसके विपरीत गाँव के जीवन में कोई भी प्रकृति को बहुत अच्छे से जान सकता है। शोर-शराबा, शहर की तंग गलियाँ जहाँ गरीब लोग रहते हैं, और भीड़ हेलेन को परेशान कर देती थी और उसे आश्चर्य होता था कि यहाँ अमीरों और गरीबों में इतना अंतर क्यों है। वह नहीं समझ पाती थी कि लोग इतने भौतिकवादी (आनंद लेने वाले) क्यों हैं और भाग्यशाली लोग गरीब भाईयों की मदद क्यों नहीं करते।

संग्रहालय और कला भंडार

हेलेन को अपनी Bicycle (साइकिल) पर घूमना बहुत पसंद था और उसके पास बहुत से कुत्ते भी थे, जब वह साइकिल चलाने या घूमने के लिए जाती थी, तो वो भी उसके साथ जाते थे। वर्षा के दिनों में वह घर के अंदर ही खेला करती थी। हेलेन का व्यवहार मित्रतापूर्ण था और उसे दूसरे बच्चों का साथ अच्छा लगता था। वह उन्हें कहानियाँ सुनाती और उन्हें अलग-अलग तरह के खेल सिखाती। कला संग्रहों में जाकर Greek (ग्रीक) देवी-देवताओं को छूकर उनकी धड़कनें महसूस करने में उसे असीम आनंद प्राप्त होता था।

हेलेन को अकेलापन महसूस होना

कभी-कभी हेलेन को अपनी जिंदगी में एक अकेलापन-सा महसूस होता था, जिससे ऐसा लगता मानो किसी बर्फ की एक चादर से वह लिपटाई गई हो। "उम्मीद हेलेन के चेहरे पर एक मुस्कान लाती और वह अपनी उन कमियों को भूल जाती थी।"

Word Meaning

Preceeding	– पिछला		Pleasure	– खुशी
Amusements	– मनोरंजन		Varied	– अलग-अलग
Rowing	– नाव चलाना		Stern	– नाव का पिछला हिस्सा
Steer	– दिशा दिखाना		Scent	– खुशबू
Poised	– संतुलन बनाना		Contend	– प्रतियोगिता करना
Exhilarating	– खुशी देने वाला		Staunch	– भरोसेमंद
Skimming	– ऊपर से निकल जाना		Glistening	– चमकता हुआ
Imperious	– उग्र स्वभाव		Surge	– अचानक भागना
Canoeing	– नाव चलाना		Shimmer	– धीमे-धीमे चमकना
Emerge	– बाहर निकलना		Luminous	– चमकदार
Enchantment	– जादू		Chopped	– काटना
Gale	– भयंकर तूफान		Swirled	– मुड़ने वाली
Billows	– सशक्त लहरें		Tacking	– दिशा परिवर्तन
Jibbing	– रुक जाना		Wrestled	– कुश्ती करना
Impetuous	– भागदौड़		Fury	– गुस्सा
Skipper	– कैप्टन		Applause	– प्रशंसा करना
Ventured	– हिम्मत करना		Nook	– कोना
Prattle	– चहकना		Elf	– परी
Gnome	– नाटे कद का		Wily	– धूर्ततापूर्वक
Initiated	– शुरू करना		Glint	– चमकना
Bluff	– धोखा देना		Lore	– बुद्धि
Gazed	– घूर कर देखना		Linden	– एक प्रकार का पौधा
Tempest	– भयंकर तूफान		Wrung	– कष्ट देना
Prostrate	– मुँह के बल लेटना		Striven	– संघर्ष किया
Hastened	– जल्दीबाजी		Alliance	– समझौता, सहमति
Conflict	– विवाद		Meadows	– घास का मैदान
Endure	– बर्दाश्त करना		Rumble	– गहरी आवाज
Smite	– हारना		Ceaseless	– लगातार
Tramp	– घुमंतू		Multitude	– लोगों की भीड़
Dissonant	– बेरुखी भरी आवाज		Tumult	– हंगामा
Frests	– चिंताएँ		Grinding	– कूटना
Clangour	– लगातार होने वाला शोर		Panorama	– भू-दृश्य
Indignant	– गुस्सा		Condemned	– घोर निंदा करना
Hideous	– प्रतिकर्षक		Withered	– सूखा और भद्दा

Ringing	– सिकुड़ा हुआ	Grimy	– गंदा
Alleys	– पतली गलियाँ	Half-clad	– आधा–अधूरा पहनावा
Underfed	– कुपोषित	Shrink	– संकुचन
Crouch	– पैर मोड़कर बैठना	Haunt	– सताना
Gnarled	– मुझा हुआ	Scrimmages	– विवाद
Thwarted	– चिंता होना	Immense	– प्रचुर
Disparity	– असमानता		

Important Questions

Questions based on the Plot of the Chapter

Q 1. Why does the city – life sadden Helen.

शहरी जीवन से हेलेन उदास क्यों हो जाती है?

हेलेन का गाँव जाना और वहाँ समय बिताना – गाँव में प्रकृति की मेहरबानी होना – गाँव के वातावरण का हेलेन को आकर्षित करना – ग्राम्य जीवन अभाव का जीवन होना – शहरी लोगों का ग्राम्य जीवन पर उदारता न होना – शहरी वातावरण का गाँव जैसा न होना – इन कारणों से शहरी जीवन की वजह से उदासी होना।

Ans. Helen often visited countrysides during summer vacation. She loved the life at countryside so much as it was in the lap of nature. It was always surrounded by flora. The rivers and the hillsides all amused her very much. But, all these delicacies of nature were absent at the city-life part. Moreover, the folk people were usually poor, underfed, underclad and they were a victim of deprivations. City people had never heeded towards this and if had done so, the folk-lives would have been excellent. Due to the ignorance of the city people and the absence of panorama of nature Helen gets saddened.

The oddities in the life style, difference in the thoughts, abnormalities in the hue and cry of the environment made Helen think that city life was not and probably could not be as equal to the flok life. She had marvellous admiration for the lives at the countryside and it had long been cherished by her.

Q 2. Why did museums and art stores give Helen immense pleasure?

संग्रहालय और कला संग्रह से हेलेन को अपार खुशी क्यों होती थी?

हेलेन को कला से बेहद प्यार और लगाव होना – इस उन्माद ने हेलेन को कला संग्रहालय तक पहुँचाया – वह ऐसे संग्रहालयों में कला के दिलकश नमूनों को छूकर महसूस करती – महसूस करने पर उसके अतिरेक की कोई सीमा न होती – ऐसे पलों को हृदय में समेटकर रख लेती।

Ans. As it is known that Helen could neither see nor hear. She would touch something and then try to recognise that thing. She had developed a great interest and affinity for art and that lead to the way of art stores and to the museums.

At these places she would get to know the beauty of art and the ability of art to quench the thirst of Helen. She would be allowed to touch the specimen there and she indulged herself in doing the activity. Yet, she couldn't see the piece of art but by touching them, she would get the idea of how it would be actually.

Helen got immense pleasure when anything valuable could be percepted by the touch of that object. Museum house for a lot of such kind of items therefore by touching them Helen must have got that pleasure underlying it. She had been truly fond of all that. There were no limits of happiness whenever Helen succeeded in doing so.

Q 3. Helen felt helpless and lonely at times. How did she overcome this?

कभी-कभी हेलेन को अकेलापन और मददहीन होने का आभास होता था। हेलेन इस पर कैसे विजय प्राप्त करती थी?

आमतौर पर मिस सुलिवान का हेलेन के साथ होना – जब मिस सुलिवान हेलेन के साथ न होती तो अकेलेपन का दौर शुरू होता – हेलेन के बाल मित्र उसके काम आते थे – हेलेन उनके साथ खेलती और उसका मन लगा रहता था – हेलेन को अलग-अलग प्रकार के खेलों का ज्ञान – इन खेलों में शामिल होकर भी वह अपना मन बहला लेती थी।

Ans. Usually, Helen remains in the company of Miss Sullivan and she would be pretty jolly staying with her, but often Miss Sullivan would not be available to her. That was the time when Helen felt very helpless and lonely.

This would irritate her and she would be strifled by the idea of being alone ever. But, to overcome the situation, Helen had made ways. She had made friends with whom she would play and found the ultimate joy. She had the idea of many indoor games that she used when being alone. These were the measures that she was using when she felt herself helpless and alone.

A friend is the biggest requisite of one's life because he spares one's happiness and boredom both. Helen must have felt that need of a friend in her life too, because she had to remain alone at times in her life too, whenever Miss Sullivan was not with her. She, therefore, had developed some skills of gaming in herself so that she could amuse herself.

Helen Appreciates the People in Her Life

Helen was blind deaf and she met people from all walks of life. When she was asked, whether people bored her, she assumed they were referring to the nosey and pushy reporters. Helen observed that the touch of hands of other people can be friendly, warm or cold and alien. A hearty handshake or a friendly letter gave Helen genuine pleasure.

Helen Met Bishop Brooks

Helen feels honoured and privileged to have met and conversed with many men of genius. Bishop Brooks was one such person. He said, 'There is only one religion, the religion of love'. Bishop Brooks believed in the fatherhood of God and the brotherhood of man.

Helen Met Famous Author and Poet

Helen also remembered Dr Oliver Wendell Holmes fondly. He was an American professor and author. Another American poet, John J Whittier too had a special place in Helen's heart. Dr Edward Hale was one of Helen's oldest friends and his wise, tender sympathy had been a support of Miss Sullivan and Helen in times of trial.

हेलेन का अपने जीवन में आए लोगों की प्रशंसा करना

Blind and Deaf (अंधी और बहरी) होने के बावजूद भी Helen (हेलेन) ने अपने जीवन में सभी प्रकार के व्यक्तियों से मिलने का सौभाग्य प्राप्त किया है। जब उससे पूछा गया कि क्या लोग उसे बोरियत का अहसास कराते हैं, तो उसने समझा कि पत्रकार लोगों की बात की जा रही है। हेलेन को आभास था कि अन्य लोगों के हाथों का स्पर्श मित्रवत, गर्म या ठण्डा और भिन्न हो सकता है। किसी से हार्दिक रूप से हाथ मिलाना या मैत्रीपूर्ण पत्र हेलेन को अपार खुशी देता था।

बिशप ब्रूक्स से हेलेन की मुलाकात

हेलेन अनेक महान् और उत्तम कोटि के व्यक्तियों से मिलकर व उनके साथ बातें करके स्वयं को गौरवान्वित महसूस करती है। Bishop Brooks (बिशप ब्रूक्स) ऐसे ही एक व्यक्ति थे। उन्होंने कहा कि 'केवल एक ही धर्म है– प्रेम का धर्म'। बिशप ब्रूक्स को भगवान के Fatherhood of God and the Brotherhood of Man (पितृत्व एवं व्यक्तित्व के भ्रातृत्व) में विश्वास था।

हेलेन की मुलाकात प्रसिद्ध लेखकों व कवियों से

हेलेन को Dr Oliver Wendell Holmes (डॉ ओलिवर वेन्डेल हॉलम्स) भी भली-भाँति याद थे। वह एक अमेरिकन प्रध्यापक तथा लेखक थे। अन्य अमेरिकन कवि, John J Whittier (जॉन जे वाइटियर) के लिए भी हेलेन के मन में एक विशेष स्थान था। Dr Edward Hale (डॉ एडवर्ड हेल) हेलेन के पुराने मित्रों में से एक थे और उनकी विवेकशील दयालुता ने Miss Sullivan (मिस सुलिवान) तथा Helen (हेलेन) का परीक्षा के समय में उनका साथ दिया।

Word Meaning

Enrich	– परिपूर्ण करना		Ministered	– ध्यान रखना
Influence	– प्रभाव		Immortal	– अमर
Ennobled	– अच्छे नैतिक मूल्य देना		Brimful	– पूरा–पूरा भरा होना
Sympathy	– सहानुभूति		Impatient	– अधीर
Essence	– जरूरत		Divine	– पवित्र
Perplexities	– उलझनें		Unpleasant	– खुशनुमा न होना
Solemn	– पवित्र		Mellow	– कोमल और मुलायम
Discontent	– असंतोष		Healing	– प्यार भरा
Brine	– नमकीन पानी		Inopportune	– कभी भी आ धमकना
Hypocricy	– जागरूक न होना		Exasperating	– परेशान करने वाला
Dumbly	– चुपचाप		Eloquent	– जो अपनी बात खुलकर कहे
Impertinence	– क्रूर		Frosty	– ठंडा
Conversed	– बातचीत करना		Clasp	– पकड़ना
Blended	– मिलाना		Insight	– अंत: ज्ञान
Dogma	– सिद्धांत		Consoles	– सांत्वना देना
Worsted	– हराना		Triumph	– जीत लेना
Cherished	– प्यार से याद करना		Lapse	– कमी
Endearment	– प्यार जताना		Benediction	– आशीर्वाद देना
Genial	– मित्रवत		Glowed	– चमक उठना
Crackled	– जोर की आवाज करना		Murmur	– धीमी आवाज में बोलना
Odour	– खुशबू		Instinctively	– उसी क्षण में
Distressed	– निराश होना		Courtesy	– इज्जत,सौजन्य से
Quaint	– आकर्षक		Slave	– गुलाम
Crouching	– घुटनों के बल बैठना		Fetters	– जंजीर

Important Questions

Questions based on the Plot of the Chapter

Q 1. Why was Bishop Brooks special for Helen? How did he clear her thoughts on religion?

बिशप ब्रूक्स हेलेन के लिए खास क्यों थे? धर्म से जुड़ी हुई हेलेन की शंकाओं का निवारण वह कैसे करते थे?

बिशप ब्रूक्स का एक असाधारण इंसान होना – बचपन से ही हेलेन पर उनका प्रभाव होना – बिशप का उसे ईश्वर के बारे में बताना – बिशप ने बताया कि सर्वमान्य धर्म प्यार है – इंसानों से अपनापन जताना – इंसान को परमपिता की सत्ता में यकीन करना दिलाना – एक-दूसरे से प्रेम करना सिखाना।

Ans. Bishop Brooks was an extraordinary person and he was really special for Helen. He had very strong influence on Helen since her childhood.

He would teach her about spiritualism and the existence of God. Brooks used to say her that there was only one religion despite of all other religions and that religion is love. It is Universal in nature and it attracts all the men who come in its way.

He preached her that everybody should believe in the fatherhood of God and there must be feeling of brotherhood in men. If these two persists then the world would be heaven and joy comes naturally.

Bishop was really a gem for Helen. He had been truly successful in planting the seed of spiritualism and humanatism in Helen. His preachings were very valuable to her and she had confined in all these as a scripture.

She had believed the words of the Bishop and whole life she had followed it. So, Bishop Brooks holds a valuable place in Helen's life.

$\mathbf{Q}$uestion $\mathbf{D}$igest

Term II

Questions Based on the Plot of the Chapter

Q 1. How did Helen get interested in learning Latin, since she was initially rather unwilling to study it?

शुरू में दिलचस्पी न होने के बाद भी हेलेन ने लैटिन भाषा सीखने में कैसे दिलचस्पी दिखाई?

Ans. At first, Helen was rather unwilling to study Latin grammar as it seemed absurd to waste time. Analysing every word, she came across - noun, genitive, singular, feminine when its meaning was quite plain. She thought that she might as well describe her pet in order to know it —order-vertebrate; division- quadruped; class -mammalia; genus -felinus; species - cat; individual -Tabby. But as she got deeper into the subject, Helen became more interested and the beauty of the language delighted her.She often amused herself by reading Latin passages, picking up words she understood and tried to make sense of them. She, thereafter never stopped enjoying this pastime. Once she was familiar with the rules of Latin grammar, she admired the language and felt that nothing was more beautiful than the language and with a tutor like Mr Irons and a dedicated teacher, Miss Sullivan, Helen could read Caesar's 'Gallic War'.

Q 2. How did Helen spend her two years in New York?

हेलेन ने न्यूयॉर्क में अपने दो साल कैसे बिताए?

Ans. Helen's two years in New York were happy ones and she looked back at them with real pleasure. She had come to New York in October 1894 to join the Wright Humason School for the deaf, accompanied by Miss Sullivan.This school was chosen especially for the purpose of obtaining the highest advantages in vocal culture and training in lip-reading.Helen also studied in the school arithmetic, physical geography, French and German. Miss Reamy, her German teacher, could use the manual alphabet and after

Helen learned some German words, they talked together in German and in a few months Helen could understand almost everything she said. Before the end of the first year, Helen read "Wilhelm Tell", a play by the German playwright, Friedrich von Schiller, with great delight. Helen studied French with Madame Olivier, a French lady who did not know the manual alphabet and who was obliged to give her instruction orally. Helen found French more difficult than German but managed to read "Le Medicin Malgre Lui". Helen was training for lip-reading and speech, but her ambition was to speak like other people.Helen studied arithmetic, which she was not too fond of and physical geography, which was a joy to learn, especially the secrets of nature. Helen also enjoyed her daily walk in Central Park where she loved to have it described every time she entered it.

Q 3. What were the disadvantages for Helen at Cambridge School ? How did Helen overcome them?

कैम्ब्रिज स्कूल में हेलेन के लिए क्या-क्या दिक्कतें थीं और हेलेन ने उन दिक्कतों का सामना कैसे किया?

Ans. At Cambridge School, the plan was to have Miss Sullivan attend the classes with Helen and interpret to her the instructions given . Her instructors had no experience in teaching pupils with disabilities and Helen's only means of conversing with them was reading their lips. However, Miss Sullivan could not spell out in Helen's hand all the books required and it was very difficult to have textbooks embossed in time to be of use to Helen, although her friends in London and Philadelphia were willing to hasten the work. For a while, infact Helen had to copy her Latin in Braille so that she could recite with the other girls. Soon, her instructors became familiar enough with Helen's speech and were able to answer her questions readily and correct mistakes. Though, Helen could not make notes in class or write exercises, she wrote all her compositions and translations at home on her typewriter.

Miss Sullivan too had to work equally hard. Each day she went to class with Helen and spelled into her hand with infinite patience all that the teachers said. In the study hours, she had to look up new words for Helen and read and re-read notes and books which Helen did not have in raised print. The difficulty of that work is hard to imagine.

Q 4. When Helen appeared for her final examinations for Radcliffe College, she had to face certain problems. What were these difficulties?

रेडक्लिफ कॉलेज की फाइनल परीक्षा में हेलेन को कुछ मुश्किलों का सामना करना पड़ा था। वे कठिनाइयाँ क्या थीं?

Ans. On the 29th and 30th of June,1899 Helen took the final examinations for Radcliffe College. The college authorities did not allow Miss Sullivan to read the examination papers to Helen, so Mr Eugene C Vining was employed to copy the papers for her in American Braille. He was a stranger to Helen and could not communicate with her, except by writing Braille. The proctor too was a stranger and did not attempt to communicate with Helen in any way. Though the Braille worked well within the languages,difficulties arose when it came to algebra and geometry.

Helen was familiar with all literary Braille in common use, but the various signs and symbols in geometry and algebra were different from the ones Helen was familiar with. Two days before the examination, Helen needed to learn the American notation, but in spite of her preparation, the combination of bracket, brace and radical confused her.

Q 5. Why does Helen feel that there are disadvantages of going to college?

हेलेन को ऐसा क्यों लगा कि कॉलेज जाने की भी कुछ कमियाँ हैं?

Ans. According to Helen, a college is not the place where scholars teach philosophy, but a place where the mind, which is burdened with all kinds of information and knowledge,cannot enjoy the treasures it has secured over the years. In a college, a student barely gets the time to actually think, to reflect and to talk to his mind. Free time is required to genuinely appreciate the words and thoughts of your loved poet. Thinking requires leisure time, but in college, students have regular classes to attend, notes to copy, complete their assignments or appear for examinations. All this leaves no quality time to think - entering the portals of learning one leaves the dearest pleasures- solitude, books and imagination outside.

While at college, students are always rushing for everything- one subject leads to another, one book leads to another and there is hardly an end to it. Leisure and the joy of books are better more satisfying than the joy that college education promises. Also, there is hardly any interaction between the students and the teachers as the professor is as distant as if he was speaking through a telephone. Helen feels it is far easier and much more pleasant to be taught by yourself as you have time to reflect and think than to be listening to the professor and just copying notes.

College life is a rush where one learns what one does, but fails to really understand. Thus, Helen soon discovers that college was not quite the romantic lyceum she had imagined and that there were disadvantages in going to college.

Q 6. Why did Helen prefer to read herself ?

हेलेन ने खुद से पढ़ना क्यों ज्यादा पसंद किया?

Ans. Helen refers to her books as her friends and ever since she was seven and read her first book, "Little Fauntleroy" then her true interest in books started.She depended on books not only for pleasure and for the wisdom they bring to all who read, but also for that knowledge which comes to others through their eyes and their ears. Miss Sullivan used to read to Helen, spelling into her hand little stories and poems that she knew, she would understand.However, Helen preferred reading herself as that gave her the freedom to choose the stories she wanted to read.In case, Helen wanted to hear a story a second or third time, she would have to depend on Miss Sullivan to read it out to her. So, Helen loved reading herself as it gave her the freedom to read and re-read a story or poem as many times as she wanted to. At times Helen's teacher was occupied in some other work and was unable to read to Helen.

In fact, she promised to read "Little Fauntleroy" in summer, but finally she read it to Helen only in August.It was when, once Miss Sullivan's fingers were too tired to spell more words that Helen took the book in her hands and tried to feel the letters herself. This way she experienced a subtle freedom as she was not under any compulsion whatsoever.

Q 7. Which were some of the outdoor sports Helen enjoyed?

वे कौन-कौन से बाहरी खेल थे, जो हेलेन को पसंद थे?

Ans. Since childhood, Helen had been fond of outdoor sports. When she was a little girl, she learned to row and swim and during the summer,when she was at Wrentham, Massachusetts ,she spent most of the time in her boat. She also enjoyed taking her friends for rowing whenever they visited her. Though she could not guide the boat very well, she could steer by the scent of water grasses and lilies and of bushes that grow on the shore. She used oars with leather bands, which kept them in position in the oarlocks and she knew by the resistance of the water when the oars were evenly poised.

Helen also enjoyed canoeing especially on moonlit nights. Although she could not see the moon climb up the sky behind the pines and steal across the heavens, she knew the moon was there. She would lie back among the pillows and put her hand in the water imagining the shimmer of the moonlight in the water. Sometimes a fish would slip through her fingers or a pond-lily would press on her hand. Helen knew when they came out in the open after passing under a cove or inlet as she could sense the spaciousness of the air around her.

Her favourite amusement was sailing. In the summer of 1901, Helen visited Nova Scotia and got opportunity to go to the ocean. The harbour was her joy and paradise. She thoroughly enjoyed the sails to Bedford Basin, to McNabb's Island, to York Redoubt and to North-West arm. At night, Helen spent some joyous and unforgettable moments in the shadow of the great, silent men-of-war. One day Helen had a thrilling experience.

There was a regatta in the North-West arm, in which the boats from the different worships were engaged. She went in a sail boat along with many others to watch the recess. Hundreds of little sail boats swung to and fro close by and the sea was calm. One summer Helen spent in one of the loveliest nooks of one of the most charming villages in New England. For many years Red Farm, by King Philip's Pond, the home of Mr JE Chamberlain and his family was Helen's home and she spent some happy days with them. She joined in all their children's sports and rambles through the woods and frolics in the water.

Q 8. What did Helen learn from Bishop Brooks ?

हेलेन ने बिशप ब्रूक्स से क्या सीखा?

Ans. Helen felt privileged to have met and conversed with many men of genius. She recalled how blessed she was to have been in the company of Bishop Phillips Brooks, an American clergyman and author.

It was a joy to spend time with him and as a child, Helen loved to sit on his knee and hold his great hand, while Miss Sullivan spelled into her other hand his beautiful words about God and the spiritual world.

She heard him with a child's wonder and delight. Her spirit could not reach upto that extent, but Bishop Brooks gave Helen a real sense of joy in life and she never left him without carrying away a fine thought that grew in beauty and depth of meaning as she grew.

Once, when she was puzzled to know why there were so many religions, he replied that there was one universal religion-the religion of love.

He asked her to love God with her whole heart and soul and also to love every child of God as much as ever and to remember that the possibilities of good were greater than the possibilities of evil and in this unconditional love lay the key to heaven.

Bishop Brooks' life was a happy illustration of this great truth. In his noble soul, love and widest knowledge were blended with faith that had become his understanding. He saw 'God in all that liberates and lifts, in all that humbles, sweetness and consoles'.

Bishop Brooks taught Helen no special creed or set of beliefs; but he impressed upon her mind two great ideas—the fatherhood of God and the brotherhood of man and made her feel that these truths underlie all creeds and form of worship.

God is love, God is our father, we are his children; therefore the darkest clouds will break and though right be worst, wrong shall not triumph.

Character Sketches

Helen Keller

She is the main character of the book, she is blind and deaf but even with that she doesn't show any repugnance for her state, there is much to say about her like she is very close to her family specially with his mother, because she's always like talking about what she does with them and all the stuff they have done for her, Like for example when she tells that when she was young she thought that her little sister wasn't like her mom's daughter.

She was always seeing her as an intruder or something, other remarkable thing that can be mentioned about Helen Keller is that she is always trying to improve herself like she really likes to find new ways to communicate herself, for example that summer she spent practicing her French, what I can tell about her is that she is an awesome life example.

Kate Adams Keller

According to the reading, Helen's Mother was tall, blonde and had blue eyes, she helped to the family at the cotton plantation, and was always taking care of Helen this can be deducted cause she was the one who realised that beside Helen's Illness there was something wrong on her daughter, she also tried helping her daughter by reading "American Notes" From Charles Dickens' about the awesome work that had been done with some deaf and blind children she died in 1921 from an unknown illness.

Arthur H. Keller

Helen's father, in the story there is not too much about him, but what can be known of him is that he is a captain who married Kate Adams (Helen's Mother) and when they started living as a couple. He owned a cotton plantation and was the editor of a weekly newspaper. He was always taking care of his daughter, Helen liked a lot when he told some stories to her.

चरित्र चित्रण

हेलेन केलर

Helen (हेलेन) इस उपन्यास की मुख्य चरित्र है। वह सुन और देख नहीं सकती, पर इसके बावजूद भी उसने इसे अपनी कमी के तौर पर नहीं व्यक्त किया। उसके बारे में कहने को बहुत कुछ है, पर वह सबसे करीब अपने परिवार के थी और खासकर अपनी माँ के। हेलेन अपनी माँ की चर्चा हमेशा करती और उन सभी का जिक्र करती, जो हेलेन ने अपनी माँ की तरफ से महसूस किया था। शुरूआत में हेलेन को उसकी छोटी बहन उसकी जिंदगी में एक अनावश्यक दखल के तौर पर महसूस हो रही थी।

हेलेन को यह भी लगता था कि वह उसकी माँ की बेटी की तरह नहीं है। हेलेन हमेशा ही अपनी जिंदगी में एक तरक्की की गुंजाइश समझती और इसके लिए पूरी जिंदगी प्रयास जारी रहा। Languages (भाषाओं) का ज्ञान भी हेलेन की सतत जद्दोजहद रही थी। वास्तव में वह एक बेहतरीन उदाहरण थी।

केट एडम्स केलर

Kate Helen (केट हेलेन) की माँ थीं और वे लंबी तथा खूबसूरत महिला थीं। घर के सभी कामों में वे मदद करती थीं और हेलेन का हमेशा से ही ख्याल रखती थीं। हेलेन की शारीरिक अक्षमता की वजह से भी उसकी माँ उसका खास ख्याल रखती थीं और यह स्वाभाविक भी था। हेलेन की माँ ने उसकी हर संभव मदद करनी चाही, ताकि हर अक्षमता को पार कर वह शिक्षा का स्वाद चख सके। हेलेन की उस बीमारी का निदान भी उसकी माँ की वजह से ही संभव हो पाया।

आर्थर एच. केलर

Arthur Keller (आर्थर केलर) हेलेन के पिता थे। कहानी में उनके बारे में बहुत चर्चा तो नहीं है, पर हेलेन की जिंदगी में उनका योगदान भी कम नहीं था। वे सेना में Captain (कैप्टन) थे तथा अपनी पत्नी के साथ रूई की पैदावार का काम देखते थे। वे एक साप्ताहिक अखबार में संपादक के तौर पर काम करते थे। वे अच्छे कथाकार थे और हेलेन उन्हें बहुत पसंद करती थी।

Mr Anagnos

Mr Anagnos was the director of the Perkins Institution. He sent Anne Sullivan to the Kellers' home. He and Keller became friends, and he had her sit on his knee when she visited the Institution. When Keller wrote "The Frost King," she sent it to him for his birthday, but because Mr Anagnos came to believe that she intentionally plagiarised it, the friendship was forever ruined.

मि. एनाग्नॉस

Mr Anagnos (मि. एनाग्नॉस) Perkins Institute (परकिंस इंस्टीट्‌यूट) में निदेशक थे। उन्होंने ही मिस सुलिवान को केलर के घर भेजा था। वे और केलर अच्छे मित्र बन गए थे। जब भी एने परकिंस जाती, तो मि. एनाग्नॉस उसे प्यार से अपनी गोद में बिठाते थे। जब एने ने The Frost King ('द फ्रॉस्ट किंग') लिखी, तो उसे एनाग्नॉस के जन्मदिन पर भेंट किया था। बाद में एने पर जब साहित्यिक चोरी का आरोप लगा था, तो एनाग्नॉस और एने के बीच की मित्रता टूट गई थी।

Dr Graham Bell

Dr Graham Bell first met Keller when she was six years old and her parents brought her to him for advice on how to teach her. Dr Bell suggested that they contact the Perkins Institution for the Blind, which they did. Dr Bell remained a friend to Keller and Anne Sullivan and accompanied them on a trip to the World's Fair.

डॉ. ग्राहम बेल

Dr Graham Bell (डॉ. ग्राहम बेल) एने से तब मिले थे जब वह मात्र छ: साल की थी और एने के माता-पिता उसकी शिक्षा के संबंध में सलाह लेने के लिए उसके पास आए थे। डॉ. बेल ने ही उन्हें परकिंस जाने की सलाह दी थी। डॉ. बेल आजीवन हेलेन व सुलिवान के मित्र बने रहे थे और विश्व मेले में भी उनके साथ गए थे।

www.ingramcontent.com/pod-product-compliance
Lightning Source LLC
Chambersburg PA
CBHW052034150726
48002CB00002B/603